Learning To Use Your Aptitudes

Learning To Use Your Aptitudes

DEAN TREMBLY, Professor
Testing and Counseling Center
California Polytechnic State University
San Luis Obispo

The Johnson O'Connor Research Foundation, Inc.

LEARNING TO USE YOUR APTITUDES

Set in 10 point Times Roman type

This volume is based on the testing and research at these locations, resulting from the work and philosophy of founder, Johnson O'Connor.

JOHNSON O'CONNOR RESEARCH FOUNDATION
HUMAN ENGINEERING LABORATORY

Atlanta, Georgia	3400 Peachtree Road, N.E., 30326
Boston, Massachusetts	347 Beacon Street, 02116
Chicago, Illinois	161 East Erie Street, 60611
Dallas-Fort Worth Area	
Irving, Texas	5525 MacArthur Blvd., 75038
Denver, Colorado	501 South Cherry Street, 80222
Houston, Texas	3200 Wilcrest, 77042
Los Angeles, California	3345 Wilshire Blvd., 90010
New York, New York	11 East 62nd Street, 10021
San Francisco, California	77 Geary Street, 94108
Seattle, Washington	1218 Third Avenue, 98101
Washington, D.C. Area	
Rockville, Maryland	600 Jefferson Plaza, 20852

CONTENTS

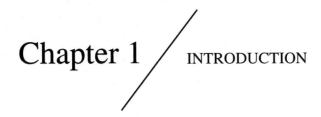

Chapter 1 / INTRODUCTION

You have taken a series of tests and know how you scored on each one. The vocabulary tests measured the amount of general and specialized knowledge that you have learned from your parents, your school, and from the world around you.

Other tests indicated your natural abilities, or aptitudes. These are thought to come from your parents or grandparents, not by learning as in the case of vocabulary, but by inheritance, as with eye color. You can't change your natural aptitudes any more than you can change the color of your eyes, but you can increase your vocabulary if you are not satisfied with it. A larger amount of knowledge generally will help you to be more successful in whatever you are doing, but a larger number of aptitudes may prove to be a handicap.

How can you put all of your aptitudes to use? It may not be easy. Unused aptitudes not only go to waste but often cause unrest and distraction. When one assembly-line worker who scored high in a test for ideaphoria was asked how he used this aptitude, he replied, "I help to organize strikes."

The aptitudes measured by the tests you have taken will be described one by one, with occasional references to combinations of aptitudes. The meaning of some low scores, as well as all high scores, will be discussed.

An inventory of aptitudes is not intended to select the one and only job for you, but if you know your abilities, you will be able to follow certain principles in making choices at each decision point during your life.

You may have wondered, before taking the aptitude and

knowledge tests, whether they would measure your "intelligence." Intelligence, however, is no longer considered to be a single thing, possessed in larger or smaller quantity by each person. A single score, a number, does not describe a human being satisfactorily. When you get a thorough medical examination, would you learn very much if you were told that your health quotient was 124? After going through a number of diagnostic tests to measure the condition and functional level of different parts of your body, you obtain specific information about each factor individually. So it is with aptitudes. The modern approach is to search for the separate variables that make up intelligence, attempt to measure them one at a time, and finally to discover what part each one plays in human behavior.

In 1922 the General Electric Company began a pioneering research program known as the Human Engineering Laboratory. The project started within the engineering department of the General Electric works at West Lynn, Massachusetts, under the direction of Johnson O'Connor. The initial purpose was to develop tests for measuring the traits characteristic of the more successful people doing different kinds of work.

Satisfactory results from the early testing of General Electric employees in the Human Engineering Laboratory led to requests for the testing of families of the employees. The increase in testing and research created the need for the laboratory to become a separate, nonprofit organization for scientific research. After leaving its industrial birthplace, the Laboratory was established for several years at the Stevens Institute of Technology in Hoboken, New Jersey, before moving into its own headquarters in New York City. Expansion of the research and testing activities to Chicago came in the 1930's, followed in 1944 by new branches in the Southwest and on the West Coast. At all but the Boston location, the work of the organization is now carried on in the name of the Johnson O'Connor Research Foundation.

Chapter 2  IDEAPHORIA

One of the very early tests administered at General Electric was for measuring the finger dexterity of meter assemblers. Other tests were designed to measure abilities thought to be of use in other departments in the company. Creative Imagination was the name given to one of the tests. Now called Ideaphoria, it measures a person's flow of ideas.

If you scored high in ideaphoria, you surely have noticed the satisfaction of finding places to use your ideas. You can find outlets for your ideaphoria in advertising, teaching, interviewing, selling, or any situation where you have a chance to talk to people, or to think up new methods, or techniques, or products.

If you scored low on a test for ideaphoria, you probably have a definite asset. A low score does not mean that you have no imagination whatever, but rather that you lack the flow of ideas characterizing those who score high. A low score indicates that you are more likely to engage in those kinds of activity where you need to concentrate and stick to facts.

If you are a student and are low in ideaphoria, you probably will make better grades in most of your subjects. English composition may cause you to stretch your thinking. If it is hard to think of a novel topic, try giving an old topic a new twist. Strive for quality instead of quantity.

Students find very few places where they can use their ideaphoria constructively. At California Polytechnic State University, where new students take a group of tests, freshmen scoring high on a test for creative thinking potential excelled in English theme composition during their first quarter with average grades of 2.21, compared with 1.79 for the low-scoring students. However, a negative relationship was found in grades for freshman biology, where the students showing the least ideaphoria on the test produced the highest grades, averaging 2.22, compared with 1.87 for those with the most imagination. The student whose ideaphoria is less active apparently finds it relatively easy to concentrate on factual subject matter.

If you lack ideaphoria, you are in the company of the majority of business executives, bankers, auditors, administrators, bookkeepers, managers, supervisors, and others whose work does not depend on the aptitude for dreaming up a constant flow of ideas.

An average or low score won't prevent you from entering an occupation where most of the people score high. Take journalism, for example, where you'll find all kinds of persons working in all kinds of specialties, some using more ideas than others. Editorial writers depend less on ideaphoria and more on analytical reasoning, an aptitude for organizing ideas into a logical sequence. Most occupations include a wide variety of workers, differing in abilities and doing a wide variety of jobs. So don't feel limited. Choose your career field, then look for places in that field where the ability to concentrate will be to your advantage.

Whether you score low or high, your best bet is to go into a field where your aptitude is not the exception. Go where you have the greatest number of chances to use your ability. It is possible but not desirable for the person with low ideaphoria to enter an idea field. Less desirable is for the idea person to enter an occupation where most of the jobs do not require ideas. But it can be done. You may be able to find the exceptional job. If you enter accounting, for example, your flow of ideas would contribute to the teaching of the subject.

A high or low score in ideaphoria or any other aptitude test does not automatically exclude you from a particular occupation; it merely indicates how you compare with the majority of people in that field. Analyze the occupation; look at a specific job. Ask yourself, "Do the activities of this job require a lot of ideas?" Knowing your aptitudes and knowing how to use them can help you make a place for yourself almost anywhere you go.

Aptitude testing was developed in educational, military, and industrial settings for the sole purpose of relating abilities to performance as students, soldiers, and employees. As the scope of the research enlarged through the years, the experience of the examinees and of those with whom they lived and worked added to the knowledge of abilities. New concepts developed. Gradually, it was realized that the aptitudes that contribute to success in engineering, accounting, production, and sales are not like so many tools, to be left in the office or shop at the end of the day. Instead, these traits are very much a part of the functioning human organism twenty-four hours a day, contributing in various ways to your behavior in any kind of situation. An aptitude, such as ideaphoria, is not like a chisel or hammer, to be picked up and used only when needed. It is more like a tool that is always in your hand, a tool that gets in your way when you're doing something that doesn't call for it. An idle aptitude can be the source of dissatisfaction, the result of conflict between the need for self-expression and the lack of opportunity to use the aptitude.

Chapter 3 / THREE-DIMENSIONAL THINKING

In several of the tests you have taken you tried to visualize some three-dimensional problems. The aptitude for structural visualization matures in the late teens and starts to decline after age 30. The ability works like a built-in computer, constantly analyzing the trajectory of objects moving through space, whether they are spacecraft or tennis balls. The work done in a number of occupations, from architecture to surgery, is performed more skillfully if you can visualize three-dimensional ideas.

Each natural mental trait is relatively independent of the other natural abilities. Having the 3-D aptitude does not mean that you also will have an active imagination. Similarly, natural abilities are independent of acquired mental abilities. A rapid flow of ideas does not always accompany a larger vocabulary. Furthermore, aptitudes appear to be independent of training and practice. Retested, experienced graduate engineers score equally as low or high on tests for spatial visualization as they did when tested originally as students.

College students who score low in structural visualization tend to major in areas such as business administration, history, languages, English, journalism, law, social science, accounting, and banking. Students who are better in structural thinking more often major in engineering, computer science, physics, chemistry, biology, astronomy, or some technical field.

Your structural visualization may be recognized by the interests you have and by how well you have enjoyed various subjects in school. However, it is possible for you to be misled by the presence or absence of a second aptitude. The low structural visualization child whose dexterity with fingers and small tools leads him to take things apart may appear to his parents as a budding engineer, while the structural child with no dexterity will not be drawn to manual activities and may avoid a three-dimensional occupation. Structural visualization is in the head, not the hands.

An artistic student, low in structural visualization, whose drawing leads to the designing of buildings, may be misled quite easily into architecture. The straight-A student, either high or low in structural visualization, being led to believe that all subjects, and therefore all careers, are equally easy, may enter an unsuitable field of work.

If you score low in structural visualization and are a student, you probably will have an easy time with the intangible aspects of most of your general courses. Only when you branch out into specialized scientific areas will you find the going more difficult. More will be said later about vocabulary and clerical speed, but these two factors, one learned and the other a natural ability, will help you learn any subject more thoroughly. The same two factors will help you succeed in some of the three-dimensional occupations, although the satisfaction you receive from your work may not equal what you might gain in a field where you are not the exception. If you already are firmly entrenched in a three-dimensional field, look around for some spot where structural visualization is not essential.

If you are a three-dimensional thinker and find yourself in a low structural visualization occupation with no desire to leave it, just start analyzing the various jobs in the field and find a place to use your ability. One life insurance salesman with the structural aptitude looked for customers among mechanics, building contractors, and engineers. A bank teller with the aptitude transferred to the loan department of the bank and became a real-estate appraiser. An English teacher transferred to a school of technology where he could teach English to future engineers and scientists.

The two sexes differ significantly in structural thinking, with only one-fourth of the women scoring higher than the average man. In genetics, the discovery of a sex difference in any trait suggests the possibility of an inheritance pattern known as sex-linked. At one time it was thought that the sex-linked pattern could be used to describe the inheritance of the aptitude for handling three-dimensional concepts. If that were the case, the presence of the trait in a son would be completely dependent on the mother. The father's aptitude would be of no consequence, but the father would have an influence on his daughter's aptitude. In this way, the aptitude would descend from father to daughter to grandson. However, later evidence suggests that if there is a sex-linked genetic factor, it is only one of several major determiners of the aptitude.

The early concept of intelligence included neither imaginative thinking nor three-dimensional thinking. The 3-D aptitude first was measured by tests of a mechanical nature, actually work samples of mechanical jobs. The tests were considered to measure practical ability or technical aptitude, not intelligence. Johnson O'Connor was one of the first to suggest that three-dimensional thinking might be an intellectual ability.

In one of the early tests, disassembled devices, such as a bicycle bell, were put together by the examinee. Test scores were used to predict the success of boys in shop courses, of machinists, sheet-metal workers, and automobile mechanics. One shortcoming of such tests was that the score depended not alone on mechanical insight but in part on manual dexterity. With the dual nature of the score in mind, the test could be used to predict success only in jobs where both visualization and dexterity were employed. Efforts of two kinds were made to correct the shortcoming of the early tests. One was to test for dexterity separately by means of repetitive manipulation of small metal pins with fingers or tweezers. The other method was to measure visualization by means of a paper and pencil test where no manipulation was required, but this method presented a new problem. It was found that scores on paper tests where time limits are imposed depend partly on clerical speed.

The University of Minnesota Spatial Relations Form Board test had a more complex shortcoming in the confusion of the 3-D aptitude with both manual dexterity and the memory for designs, or forms. The examinee was asked to place a number of cut-out pieces into matching cut-out spaces. The change to a paper test called Minnesota Paper Form Board eliminated dexterity but not the memory for design. The next step was to measure design memory and visualization in two separate tests.

You have read about the Industrial Revolution, the change in social and economic life starting in England around 1760 and later spreading to other countries. During the Industrial Revolution, hand tools and manufacture were replaced by steam-powered machine tools in large-scale industrial production. Until that time, formal schooling was devoted to philosophy and the classics. Stonemasons and carpenters learned their trades as apprentices; on-the-job training it would be called today. Only rarely did a genius like Leonardo da Vinci bridge the chasm between the artisan and the intellectual elite.

The Industrial Revolution created the need and the educational establishment slowly began to provide the training for the three-dimensional students. Boys who would have been limited to the trades now were trained to be technicians, engineers, and scientists. But enough of the elitist, classical philosophy of education remains to this day in most schools to cause difficulties for the three-dimensional thinker. In addition to the 3-D aptitude, a small vocabulary militates against success in the general, traditional curriculum. The low-achiever is too often shunted toward a technical education, a suitable direction only if he has structural visualization and dexterities. The student's aptitude pattern, not his degree of excellence as a scholar, should determine his vocational direction. Progress in that direction can be aided by a vocabulary-building program. The low structural visualization low-achiever, particularly, needs to develop vocabulary, both for vocational and educational success.

In the category of learnable intellectual factors, an inadequate vocabulary can prevent a student from a full comprehension of what he reads and hears, which in turn leads to lower grades. Likewise, a lack of background in a particular subject will cause difficulty in learning new material. At California Polytechnic State University, as at most institutions of higher education, students are placed on academic probation when their grade point average falls below 2.00. During the year of 1967-68, fifty-nine percent of the freshmen who were on probation had vocabulary age-levels below their chronological ages. In the same freshman class, those who scored below 500 in the mathematics section of the Scholastic Aptitude Test averaged 2.17 in their first-year mathematics courses, compared with an average of 3.04 for those above 500.

The handicap of a deficient general vocabulary or of specialized mathematics knowledge can be remedied simply by acquiring additional knowledge. The most efficient way to learn vocabulary is to straighten out gradually the meaning of words with which you already are slightly acquainted, the words on the frontier of your knowledge.

A handicap to learning, not so easily remedied, may come from a deficiency in one of the natural intellectual factors, or aptitudes. The lack of clerical speed, or graphoria, contributes to slowness and inaccuracies in the paper and pencil part of school work.

While the handicapping effect of slow clerical speed is present in all courses of study, other aptitudes may influence only a single area, such as a lack of pitch discrimination in the study of vocal music. There is no remedy for the vocal student, but if you are a slow clerical worker, you can compensate in various ways, and this will be discussed in a later chapter.

The absence, or lack, of an aptitude is not the only kind of learning handicap. The presence of an aptitude may act in the same way. For the past fifty years, various tests to measure structural visualization have been given to both students and adults, with the test scores showing a relation to success in the study and practice of engineering, architecture, physics, and other fields where three-dimensional thinking is needed.

At first the testers had a one-sided view of the aptitude. They saw that high-scoring persons were good in engineering and that low scorers were not good in engineering. In the second stage of their learning about the aptitude, they began to see that persons who scored low on tests for structural thinking appeared to have an advantage in fields that involve words and ideas rather than things.

As early as 1943, it was found that boys who scored high in tests for structural visualization had low grades in foreign languages compared to other subject areas. Since males average higher than females in tests for the spatial factor, it is not surprising that more males have difficulty with languages. In 1964, another study showed a negative correlation between the aptitude and grades in German. In 1972, a study made of the relation of the spatial factor to grades in French, German, Russian, and Spanish showed negative correlations. Some teachers and counselors believe that structural visualization is a handicapping factor not only in the study of foreign languages but also in the study of philosophy and other subjects where the aptitude is not challenged.

The aptitudes and interests of an author of textbooks introduce still another element into the learning situation. If the person who writes a history text has the structural aptitude, the book will be more likely to include the "hardware" aspects of historical occurrences, such as buildings and machinery.

Students who have the 3-D aptitude should not avoid a foreign language any more than low structural visualization students should avoid a course in physics as part of a general education. The students might expect to work a little harder and enjoy it less. There is little likelihood that a career choice would follow, in either case.

The presence of an aptitude other than structural visualization may act as a handicap to learning, again only in certain subjects, or in some area of a subject. A student with an active imagination, a rapid flow of ideas, can make full use of the ability when writing a theme in an English class but may be distracted by it when learning to conjugate a verb.

It is a challenge for individuals to use all their aptitudes in a single job. As a result, many-aptitude persons may find themselves changing from one job to another, searching for a place to use their idle aptitudes. They may stay in one job and pursue a number of hobbies, or they may work in an extremely small organization, possibly their own, where each day offers a variety of duties to challenge the various aptitudes. Maximum effectiveness is achieved when many-aptitude persons works toward a long-range goal with a constant challenge offered by no single, standardized job.

You can evaluate any kind of work or hobby in terms of your aptitudes by asking yourself, "Which of the activities I am considering will best use my aptitudes?" For example, does the activity use three-dimensional thinking? Does the work use a rapid flow of ideas?

Chapter 4 / DEXTERITY

The success of military psychologists in 1917-18 and during the occupational-rehabilitation movement following World War I served to spread throughout industry the aims and possibilities of employee testing. In his 1917 book, *Choosing Employees by Mental and Physical Tests*, W. F. Kemble described a test for finger dexterity as a pegboard with rows of holes in which wooden matches or metal pegs were inserted. With the pegboard, a person could demonstrate speed of filling the holes, first with one hand and then with the other.

A modification of the pegboard was used by Johnson O'Connor at the General Electric Company. In the test, three hundred standard metal pegs, an inch in length, are picked up three at a time and inserted in one hundred holes, each large enough to hold three of the pegs.

In the course of the early experiments with the finger dexterity test, several hundred women working as electric meter assemblers were asked to put the pegs in the holes. The fastest one finished in slightly less than five minutes, while another needed more than fifteen minutes to do the same test. What causes such a striking difference? Is it practice? One of the slowest performers was asked to repeat the experiment. She improved, and on the second trial needed less than thirteen minutes. Further trials, one a day for a month, produced a gradual increase in speed, although the rate of increase at the end of the month was small.

The performance of most any job improves with repetition. The ability of every person to learn by practice is often overlooked. No one ever reaches the limits of his or her capacity.

Johnson O'Connor next compared two groups of the meter assemblers. One group averaged six minutes in the finger dexterity test and the other nine minutes, half again as long. On the second trial, the nine-minute group improved, approaching eight minutes. The six-minute group also improved to about four and one-half minutes. The slow group still took half again as long as the fast group. The two groups then repeated the assembly test once a day for a month. The nine-minute group improved strikingly, requiring at the end of the month not more than six minutes. The six-minute group improved as well, needing only about four minutes. The slow group, even after that amount of practice, was still relatively slow, the fast group relatively fast.

If improvement with practice is a general law, you will go further if you practice at something in which you are naturally superior. The story of the tortoise and the hare is true only when the hare goes to sleep. You should work at something that best suits your aptitudes.

The various pioneers who designed the first generation of dexterity tests assumed a general dexterity ability. Today we recognize several independent dexterities, each useful in its own way. The early belief in a general dexterity was founded on the idea that you will use the same fingers in handling a tool as you will in picking up and handling pins or pegs.

The meter assembly work at General Electric involved the use of tweezers and small tools as well as use of the fingers. The suggestion of a woman engaged in training new employees in miniature assembly work, that a person good in the finger dexterity test might not do well in handling small tools, led to the development of the tweezer dexterity test. You can be extremely dexterous with your fingers and slow with tweezers, or the other way round. Some are fast in both and others are slow. The tweezer test is similar to the finger test except that only one pin is put in each hole, and a very small hole at that.

Cooking, washing dishes, fixing gadgets, and building things are done better and with more enjoyment if you have dexterous fingers. Dexterity of one kind or another is important to the success of assemblers, artists, craftsmen, dentists, surgeons, painters, and violinists. Your ability to succeed in any of these lines is usually a product of several independent factors, not dexterity alone. Powers of visual and tactual discrimination may be of importance, as in painting or weaving; perception of spatial relations as in sculpture; auditory acuity as in piano tuning. Knowledge of words is needed in typesetting or typewriting; musical aptitudes in a musician; understanding of anatomy and structural visualization in a surgeon; and memory for design in an artist.

If you score high in finger dexterity or in one of the other dexterity tests, try to use it in some way; in your work if possible, in a hobby if not.

Lack of education more often than lack of other aptitudes may force a young person into a job requiring manual labor, but laborers can and do advance in their organizations to positions in record-keeping, inspection work, technical operations, sales, and management. Young people with the benefit of more education often start in semi-skilled work as stepping stones to more responsible positions.

Chapter 5  SUBJECTIVE– OBJECTIVE

Is research more attractive than selling? Does the professional world attract you more than the business world? Do you prefer work of an individual nature, or do you prefer to work as a member of a group?

If you are subjective, you are more likely to achieve satisfaction through your own individual efforts, while the objective person achieves by working through other people. You will do research and write the textbook used by the objective teacher whose goal is reached through the learning of the students. You will be a private-duty nurse, while the objective person is a supervisor of nurses. You will design a new automobile to be sold by an objective salesman. Your contribution to humanity will be more indirect than that of the objective person.

You would be an exception in the world of selling, but you could succeed there by following the example of a few specialists. Sell large units: commercial jets instead of bicycles, freighters instead of rowboats. Sell repeat orders: serve as a consultant to regular customers. One insurance man who was a member of the "million dollar round table" had written that much insurance in one year by making contact not with large numbers of prospects but with fewer than a dozen.

Life is more comfortable for all concerned when executives are objective, but a person who scores subjective can get along if he enters the organization at the top (as in a family business), if he confines himself to policy matters, and if he delegates the everyday operations to an objective assistant. A subjective person can get along

15

still better in an executive post if he has low structural visualization and if both his general knowledge (English vocabulary) and specialized knowledge are superior. Promotions within an organization often create problems when the influence of aptitudes is not realized. A subjective worker who is promoted to a supervisory position because of his outstanding individual work may not be satisfied in his new role.

The objective person can succeed by isolating himself for brief periods of time. The objective journalist succeeds in writing interspersed with interviews to gain background material.

The aptitude for visualizing in three dimensions often conflicts with objectivity, for one suggests working with things while the other suggests working with people. One resolution would be to operate a structural business. Another would be to teach engineering or other 3-D subjects.

In investigating a job, ask "Is the work of an individual nature or do I need to work through other people?" Follow the principle, at each decision point in your life, of asking questions of this kind. You will find that a knowledge of your natural abilities often will assist you in making your decision.

Chapter 6  INDUCTIVE REASONING

Inductive reasoning enables you to derive a principle from a number of particular instances, to see relationships, and draw conclusions from them. If you don't have sufficient knowledge you may jump to a wrong conclusion. In fact, no aptitude is of much value without knowledge to accompany it. You are not worth much to an employer if you don't know a lot about the world around you and a lot about your chosen occupation. Both general knowledge and specialized knowledge are essential.

When something goes wrong or stops working, whether it is a human body, or a social institution, or a mechanical device, the inductive reasoning aptitude comes to the rescue. A thorough knowledge of how an automobile works, linked with inductive reasoning, makes it possible for a mechanic to diagnose the ailments of your rubber-footed steed.

Scientific research, diplomacy, critical writing, law, and medicine are examples of occupations where critical and diagnostic thinking can be an asset.

The objective person in management oversees the work of others and reaches wise decisions based on knowledge and experience rather than on snap judgments. The objective, imaginative salesman respects the customer's desires rather than diagnosing the reasons why the customer should not buy.

Being low in the diagnostic aptitude need not keep you out of the medical field. Many physicians devote their skills to the treatment of disease, leaving the diagnostic work to specialists. A superior degree of legal knowledge and general knowledge, coupled with a complete background of the client's case, may allow a person without inductive reasoning to succeed in the field of law. Legal partnerships often combine an assortment of talents and skills.

Former Chief Justice Warren Burger of the United States Supreme Court illustrates the influence of vocabulary and inductive reasoning on the practice of law. In a speech at Fordham University Law School, the Chief Justice strongly supported the need for testing and special training before a lawyer would be allowed to perform as a trial lawyer. It is true that most of the 600,000 lawyers in the United States rarely enter a courtroom. They stay in their offices drawing up contracts, wills, and divorce papers, or they work for some corporation, attending to organizational, tax and other problems.

As a result of the freedom of a lawyer to practice any kind of law, the unhappy Chief Justice said, "The courtrooms of America all too often have 'Piper Cub' advocates trying to handle the controls of 'Boeing 747' litigation." Unsure of himself and his field, the inept trial attorney often bogs down the courts with superfluous details that cover every contingency; or at the other extreme, he may sink a client's case by missing a critical point.

In the language of aptitudes, inductive reasoning is perhaps somewhat more important in courtroom work than in private practice. Essential to any kind of legal practice is a superior general background of knowledge as reflected by English vocabulary. In addition, a thorough familiarity with legal knowledge and information is demanded.

Successive steps in traditional patterns of promotion often call for opposite types of aptitudes. Many salesmen score low on tests for inductive reasoning; many sales managers score high. In one organization, the man recommended on the basis of aptitude tests to be the next sales manager (and he became a good one), had been one of the poorest salesmen.

Now you have an additional question to ask yourself at each decision point in your life, "Does the activity I am considering require diagnosis and criticism?"

Chapter 7 / CLERICAL SPEED

One of the less obvious characteristics of the eyes is the speed of eye movements, or eye focusing. Other descriptive labels that may be applied to the same trait include visual dexterity, eye dexterity, ocular motility, and visual perceptual speed. This trait is now recognized by the testing profession as an intellectual factor called Perceptual Speed. It is also recognized that the trait has many different uses. At first, however, the aptitude was considered to be useful only in vocations of a clerical or bookkeeping nature. Hence, tests for measuring the aptitude carried (and in some cases still carry) names indicative of the aptitude's first application to an occupation: Clerical Test, Clerical Ability, Clerical Aptitude Examination, Clerical Speed and Accuracy, Office Worker Test, Paper and Pencil Speed, Clerical Perception, Accounting Aptitude, and Graphoria. The latter is a coined word that means "a flow of something written."

Tests were first used in the selection of clerical workers in the early 1900's. One number-comparison test had two columns of numbers, starting at the top with two digits in each column and ending at the bottom with eleven. When the numbers across from each other in the two columns were identical, the examinee put a check mark in a third column, which was headed SAME. When the numbers were not the same, a check mark was made in a fourth column under the heading of DIFFERENT.

A test called Accounting Aptitude, similar to the one just described, was one of several tests used at General Electric to predict success in accounting. The Accounting Aptitude test, later called Graphoria, worked well for the right-handed person. But it presented difficulties to the left-handed person because both the SAME and DIFFERENT columns were on the right-hand side of the two columns of numbers. In a revision of the test, which placed a single column of lines between the two columns of numbers, the examinee made a check mark on the line in the middle column when the opposite numbers were the same.

The Accounting Aptitude test was found to be a valid predictor of success in the accounting department, both as to number of years with the company and as to advancement in the department. The aptitude is for both speed and accuracy in visual perception; it helps one to observe words, numbers, and symbols, and to see instantly what is on the paper, whether in reading or writing. Although the measurement of the aptitude and many of its uses require a pencil, the basic ability is visual. Accountants and auditors in their work will scan columns and pages of numbers without touching a pencil.

This aptitude also is related to success in the job of being a college student. It contributes to the rate of reading and to the rapid and accurate performance of the paper and pencil part of schoolwork. In 1967-68, freshmen at California Polytechnic State University were given the Clerical and Perceptual Speed test. Those whose scores were in the top 20 percent carried an average of sixteen units, or credit hours, while those in the bottom 20 percent carried 14 units. If the slow students had taken still fewer units than 14, their grade point average of 2.48 might have been closer to the 2.88 grade point average of the faster students.

Courses with a greater amount of paper and pencil work depend more on this aptitude. The quantity of written assignments, as well as the number and length of written tests in connection with a given subject, relate not only to the nature of the subject matter but also to the policy of the instructor or institution. In general, learning depends more on the clerical aptitude in the larger classes, the larger schools, and the larger cities. The one-room school of the past did have its advantages.

Boys are not only two to three years behind girls in the development of this ability, but they still are slower than girls when the aptitude becomes fully mature around the age of thirty. In genetics, a sex difference in any trait suggests the possibility of an inheritance pattern known as sex-linked. With fewer than 25 percent

20

of the males scoring above the female median, the aptitude may prove to be a sex-linked trait. Neither training and experience in clerical work nor the acuity of the eyes influence the performance on the test. The sighting eye also is independent of the aptitude.

In the Number Checking part of the Minnesota Clerical Test, with a time limit of eight minutes, the fastest boys complete more than twice as many items as the slowest boys, and the fastest girls outdo the slow ones in the same ratio. These extreme ranges are not apparent in the classroom when knowledge of the subject matter is paramount and when no written work is involved.

A simple experiment will identify the slow students in any class and illustrate their learning handicap. Ask the students to work for five minutes on a page of short, simple addition problems, or an elementary vocabulary test, or any kind of easy test where all of the answers are known perfectly, where knowledge is not being measured. Ask the students to go at their greatest possible speed and to hold up their hands when they have finished.

If everyone is allowed to complete the test, the slowest ones will take about twice as long as the fast ones. If time is called when the fast ones have reached the end, the slowest ones will be about halfway through. When an examination on actual subject matter is so long that only a few in the class have time to complete it, the instructor is measuring two things: knowledge of the subject matter and speed of doing paper work. This is one way to measure the aptitude, but it is not the best way.

Norms are furnished with published tests, but meaningful application of results from any test requires the use of local norms. A student with a learning problem needs to be compared with others in the same group.

Some teachers and schools have developed their own tests. California Polytechnic State University uses a short, three-digit number comparison test to measure perceptual speed. The first part of the instructions is given below.

"By rapidly comparing pairs of three-digit numbers, you can determine your clerical and perceptual speed. Examples are given below. A check mark is put on the line when the two groups of digits are the same. You will notice that the numbers on about half of the lines are the same and that these lines have been checked."

Examples:

692	√	692
241		248
526		326
179		579
837	√	837
273		293
638	√	638
859	√	859
594		596
462	√	462

After viewing a full column of examples, the student practices on a second column, then goes to the test itself. The test consists of two pages, with three columns on each page, for a total of 180 items. Top speed is requested and two minutes are allowed.

A device called the eye camera is designed to photograph the eye movements involved in reading. It is quite possible that a measurement of perceptual speed can be made with the eye camera. Two other simple techniques offer additional means of measuring the speed of perceiving visual stimuli without the use of a paper and pencil test. One is called Flicker Fusion. When a person views a light through spaces in a rotating shutter, a flicker is perceived at low rates of rotation. As the rate of rotation is increased gradually, the examinee can report the point where the flicker disappears. The fusion threshold, where the flicker fuses into a steady light, is fairly stable for each person in repeated trials and there are great individual differences.

In a similar technique, demonstrating what is called Apparent Movement, two lights side by side are exposed alternately by shutters. As the speed of exposure is increased, a point is reached where the examinee sees apparent movement of a single light going back and forth. Further increase in speed brings the examinee to a second threshold where the apparent movement disappears and two steady lights are seen. There is a wide range of individual differences.

If you are a student and you are slow in perceiving, the new awareness of why you may be slow in school can bring a major improvement in your self-concept. You will realize that you are not slow, only your eyes are slow. If you are a teacher, the new awareness of this little known factor in learning will help you to understand the students in your classes who are not dexterous with their eyes. If you are a student, compensate in your learning efforts by increasing your vocabulary. Overlearn each subject. Ask questions. Take an active part in class discussions. Talk with your teachers about your slowness. If the problem persists, try to move to a small, private school. If you are a boy, go to a school for boys where you will have no competition from the faster sex. Not many girls are handicapped by slowness in visual perceptual speed, but if you are one of them and are attending a school for girls, you probably would do better in a coed school, where you would have some slower boys as classmates.

Attend a small college. Carry fewer units. Make use of tape recorders and calculators. Push as rapidly as possible through your paper assignments in order to overcome the natural tendency to be overly cautious. Improve your study habits. Adopt a positive attitude.

If you are a teacher, measure the visual speed of all of your students. Among those who show a slowness in perceptual speed, how many also have a learning problem? Analyze your teaching methods. Is the homework load too heavy, particularly for the boys? Do you keep this aptitude in mind when designing your examinations so that even the slowest students have enough time to complete all of the items? If there is need to keep the faster students busy during the entire test period for the sake of order in the classroom, an additional number of noncredit, difficult items may be placed at the end of the test for them to do.

Lack of the aptitude prevents many students from gaining a formal education that is commensurate with their abilities. Potential engineers may end up as mechanics, and potential teachers may settle for a place in retail merchandising. This is a waste of human resources, but it is still more devastating to the individual who is forced to wear the brand of a dropout or underachiever. A follow-up study of individuals who as high school seniors eight years earlier were tested on the DAT Clerical Speed and Accuracy subtest, showed a striking relation of the aptitude to educational attainment. Those who received an advanced degree averaged at the 75th percentile in clerical speed; 71 was the average for college graduates, 58 for those who did some college work, 49 for those who attended special schools (art, business, technical), and 38 for the ones with no higher education.

Slowness can hinder even the high-vocabulary student who learns concepts easily but who falls behind in the "bookkeeping" part of his learning. The lack of the aptitude is not only a disadvantage in the actual doing of the paper work, but it acts as a deterrent to the starting of any lesson preparation. In this case, the lack of the aptitude functions as negative motivation.

While only some of the world's work depends on the speed and accuracy of using paper and pencil, nearly all of the work you do in school depends on it. Once you clear the hurdle of your formal education, you will find that the worst is over. If you have slow eyes that don't readily perceive the small details, you will be able to comprehend the whole picture more clearly. Don't let yourself become bogged down in details. Deliberately focus on the total situation in your study and in your work. Try to see the big picture.

Being adept at paper work can have its disadvantages, too. One who relies on speed often neglects the mastery of the subject matter. The fast student who sails through every subject without a hitch, being led to believe that all subjects, and therefore all careers, are equally easy, may enter an unsuitable field of work. If he is fortunate in choosing a compatible occupation, his speed and accuracy in doing the paper work of the entry job in his field may earmark him as an efficient clerical worker and prevent his advancement to more responsible and suitable positions.

There are other sources of learning problems. Inadequate vocabulary provides no foundation of knowledge on which to build, no concepts with which to combine new material. Improper attitudes toward school and ignorance of productive study methods handicap some students.

Lack of an aptitude for a special field of study often is a problem. Students who major in architecture are severely handicapped without the natural ability to visualize in three-dimensions. The aptitude is related to high grades in a number of specific courses required in architecture: perspective, design, delineation, strength of materials, analytic geometry, calculus, and physics.

All learning problems are serious matters. Slowness in perceptual speed is not only one of the greatest problems; it also is one of the least recognized among teachers and students. It can be a handicap not only in the learning of academic subjects but also in learning to read multiple-staff piano and organ music.

Chapter 8 / NUMBER FACILITY AND NUMBER SERIES

In many everyday situations, it is helpful to be able to do arithmetic quickly in your head. Most of us have probably noticed that when several people split the bill at a restaurant, there is often one person who naturally takes on the task of figuring out how much each person owes, and how much the tip should be. When traveling in foreign countries, some people immediately assimilate the exchange rate and can calculate how much something would cost in their own currency, while others are left to fumble with a calculator.

The Number Facility test measures this sort of "computational speed" by challenging you to rearrange chips with numbers on them so that they form correct addition and multiplication equations. It is the sort of test on which virtually all examinees can get the correct answers; a high score, however, indicates greater speed in getting there.

What sorts of jobs and careers would provide an outlet for quickness with arithmetic? It could be an asset in almost any facet of the business world. It could speed up the work of the accountant and bookkeeper. It could help the salesperson who has to formulate quick estimates and calculate discounts on the spot. It could also be an asset for a bank teller or ticket seller when it's necessary to count money and provide change quickly in order to serve a rapid flow of customers.

The Number Series test, in which you had to find the pattern in a string of numbers in order to complete the sequence, indicates a talent for using numerical information to solve problems. This trait points to fields that include analysis of financial or other numerical data—for example, economics, finance, tax law, and computer science. In the social sciences, it points to statistical analysis for sociological or psychological research, or the study of demographics for marketing or public health studies. Most areas of science and engineering offer constant opportunities to analyze numbers.

Numerical traits alone may not dictate your career choice. But if you score high in one or more numerical traits, look for chances in any field you choose to tackle numerical problems. If you are a doctor or nurse, you might be interested in epidemiological studies. If you are inclined toward sales, consider getting training to be a stockbroker or financial planner. Even artistic fields could provide an outlet for numerical traits. The study of music theory and composition, for example, may involve working with repeating numerical patterns. And in the art world, a head for numbers could be an asset in auction work or in calculating values for insuring art exhibits.

A word of caution: If you scored low in Graphoria (see chapter 7), you may find your enjoyment of numerical problem-solving ceases when it comes to the paper-and-pencil work. We would not suggest areas where the main emphasis is on keeping track of numbers accurately, as in bookkeeping. Instead, look for situations where you need to think with numbers and discuss estimates and financial strategies, but have an accountant, secretary, or research assistant handle the clerical aspects of the job.

Chapter 9  MEMORY FOR NUMBERS

When you dial the information operator from a pay phone, are you confident that you will be able to remember the number you get long enough to dial it? Do the numbers you see on license plates tend to stick in your mind even though you do not try to remember them? Do sports statistics, or stock quotations, or historical dates stick in your mind? Some people have the ability to remember numbers quickly regardless of their interest in them.

In the test for number memory, six-digit numbers are flashed rapidly on a screen one at a time. After eight different numbers are shown, the examinee recalls as many numbers as possible. These same eight numbers are shown a second, third, and fourth time, always in a different sequence. After even such a brief viewing, people with a strong natural ability remember numbers that have no apparent meaning.

In the past, some people were thought to have a "good memory." This seems to be inaccurate. A person with low memory for numbers may be fast at recalling words. It seems that instead of saying a person has a good memory, one must specify a memory for what. Many different kinds of memory already are measurable, and research will uncover still others. Perhaps some people remember faces more readily, or odors, or colors. Actually, the possibilities seem endless.

With all the numbers that are used in modern life—Social Security numbers, banking identification, telephone numbers, addresses—a strong memory for numbers can certainly be useful. People in mathematics, computer programming, engineering, and the sciences need to remember numbers, equations, and formulas. Police officers and investigators need to remember license-plate numbers. Travel and ticket agents find it helpful if they can remember fares and timetables. Numbers are the very essence of the stock market and inventory control. Scheduling of classes for a school or flights for an airline, editing a newspaper or magazine, managing a wholesale or retail business—all are done more efficiently if one has a memory for numbers.

If you score low in tests for number memory, please do not abandon hope! Use references. Write down the telephone numbers that you get from information.

Make a note of stock numbers or sales quotations. Carry your Social Security card with you. Try looking at the positive side—you won't have people avoiding you at parties because you are constantly reciting new sports statistics.

As with other aptitudes, if you do have a strong memory for numbers and are not using it constructively, try to adjust your work to use it. There is, however, a caution. Many of the jobs involving memory for numbers also require keeping exact records; speed in doing paper-and-pencil work may also be necessary.

Chapter 10 / ART

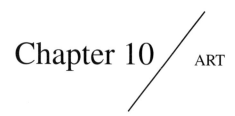

In the Memory for Design test, you look for 12 seconds at a collection of straight lines running at different angles, some connected with others and some parallel. The design is purposely abstract, resembling nothing identifiable. Then, from memory you try to connect the dots on a sheet of paper to form the same design.

Since your memory for design is fully mature by the time you are 15, your professional art training should be in full swing by that time if you want to take full advantage of your ability. Your experience and increased knowledge will compensate for any slight decrease in memory as you grow older.

Design memory is the aptitude that helps you to remember the styles of clothing and the designs of automobiles. Some musicians memorize by a kind of mental photography which enables them to recall the image of the printed sheet of music. In remembering a particular passage in a book, certain individuals can tell you that it was "at the top of the right-hand page." Some painters sit in their studios and paint scenes from their memory storage; others prefer to paint while looking at their subjects.

Without some imagination and dexterity to handle the tools of the trade, your memory for design may not motivate you to any kind of creative art. With imagination and dexterity but without the individualized motivation of the subjective person, your creative efforts may not reach the peak of the art world, but you might still probably gain a feeling of satisfaction by using your aptitudes.

Beyond the field of art, your memory for the shape of things can be a contributing factor to your success in museum work, photography, or advertising. In architecture and engineering, the memory ability plays a secondary role to the primary factor of structural visualization. Whether or not you have a good memory for designs, just knowing that there is a special ability of this kind will increase your understanding of yourself and others.

If you are a man, are you one of the five out of a hundred who cannot tell some colors apart? The visual deficiency known as color blindness is even more infrequent in women. There are types and degrees of color blindness. Some men cannot discriminate between red and green while others confuse yellow and blue.

Color perception is essential to artists and to others who need to distinguish one color from another. What essential use could be found for color blindness? An answer was found during World War II when it was discovered that a color-blind airman on a survey mission was able to spot the enemy artillery installations disguised by canvas painted to resemble trees. The colored canvas fooled everyone but the new hero who distinguished the difference in textures between the real and the imitation treetops. The incident proved to be embarrassing to the man, for he had gained admission to the Air Force by deception. He had learned the nature of the colored-dot test for color perception and had memorized the correct responses. However, he not only was forgiven, but the Air Force immediately sought additional color-blind men to assist in this essential activity.

An incident in civilian life illustrates another use for color blindness, that of matching colors. This, too, was discovered by accident. On a sunny day in October many years ago, an affluent man traded in his gas guzzler on a new model. He drove the car home and proudly parked it in the driveway in full view of his envious neighbors. His best friend, who happened to be color-blind, came across the street to offer congratulations. The friend walked around the car and then made a comment that the paint on the right front fender didn't match the rest of the car. Different colors appear as different shades of gray to the color-blind person. Further inspection under the car revealed a carefully straightened brace. The car obviously had been in an accident and the paint for the fender had not been perfectly matched. The dealer, on being confronted with the evidence, readily admitted that on a trial run his son had hit an immovable object. The car actually was as good as new, but in retribution the dealer reduced the price of the car to the factory wholesale cost.

Since the incidents of the camouflage and the wrecked car, it has been learned that one paint factory employs a color-blind man who double-checks the paint mixers on every newly mixed batch of paint.

Chapter 11 / AUDITORY ABILITIES

Music, the universal language, is a first in three ways. It is the first of the measurable aptitudes that are likely to have developed in human evolution; first to develop in the individual; and first to be measured objectively. Recognition, discrimination, and memory of sounds must have appeared very early in the evolutionary growth of our ancestors.

Pitch discrimination and the memory for tunes, called tonal memory, are the earliest maturing of all measurable aptitudes. Ten-year-olds score nearly as high as adults on group tests where the answers must be written. Sound comes before sight in the newborn infant, and musical aptitudes are the first to be recognized and encouraged by parents.

Objective tests to measure musical aptitudes were among the first to be developed. Carl E. Seashore began to work out his Measures of Musical Talent at the University of Iowa in 1901. For centuries before his time, it had been apparent that certain individuals possess the musical gift to a greater degree than do most of their fellow beings. But before Seashore, the musical gift had been thought of as a single, unitary talent for music. Seashore shattered that long-held belief when he demonstrated that talented musical performance depends not only on several distinct musical factors but on some other aptitudes as well.

Seashore's innovative concept of the multifactor nature of musical talent blazed the trail for other psychologists to follow in their study of other human abilities. His work led to research that answered the puzzling question of how one person, after an equal amount of training on both instruments, could master the violin but not the piano, while a second person under the same conditions would do much better on the piano.

Seashore's testing and research led in 1919 to the issue of his Measures of Musical Talent on phonograph records. Further research led to a revision of the Measures of Musical Talent so that it also included tonal memory and rhythm memory, together with measures for the discrimination of pitch, time, loudness, and timbre (tonal quality).

Included in the hundreds of studies made since Seashore's Measures were first introduced have been research on the inheritance of musical traits, the relationship between capacity and achievement in music schools, the relationship between faulty speech and the lack of some of the musical traits, and surveys of musical talent in public schools.

Beyond the purely musical applications, the Measures have been used in physics experiments, in the examination of prospective physicians for some of their work, and in warfare for the selection of persons best equipped to locate enemy submarines. A musical deputy sheriff who spent much of his time in a patrol car on the wide country roads of West Texas said that he could judge the speed he was traveling within three miles an hour by the sounds of the motor and the tires on the road.

Earmindedness appears to be related to electronics engineering and learning to speak foreign languages. One woman had learned to distinguish and remember the variations in the spoken language in various parts of the United States where she had travelled with her husband on business trips. Hearing a few words, she could tell from what part of the country a person hailed. At the time she took the aptitude tests she was able to speak Spanish and was planning to learn French.

While an ear for music may help you learn the sounds of a foreign language, the way a language looks may be learned with the help of a different kind of memory. As long ago as 1885, Hermann Ebbinghaus, the renowned German experimental psychologist, studied the ability of individuals to memorize verbal material. He used nonsense syllables, short made-up words, to avoid the influence of previous learning that would be present in using ordinary words. He performed a series of classic experiments on himself in which he learned a number of nonsense syllables well enough to recite the list perfectly. Then, after varying rest intervals, he measured the time it took to relearn the list. He found that he had forgotten 47 percent of the material during the first 20 minutes, 66 percent during the first day, and 79 percent after 31 days.

Meaningful material is, of course, retained longer. Poetry is remembered better than prose. Material learned on the basis of insight, such as the working of a puzzle or the way to do a card trick, may show very long retention.

Nonsense syllables, found to be an excellent and accurate research device, have been used widely in research on learning since their initial use in the late 1800's by the German psychologist Hermann Ebbinghaus. Kim Margolis, a staff member of the Human Engineering Laboratory in the 1940's, made up a list of nonsense syllables and called it the Silogram test, an apt title that uses her last name spelled backwards.

Designed in the form of paired associates, the Silogram test consists of a series of twenty slides, each containing two words, one a real word and the other a pronounceable made-up word. You are shown the slides one at a time. Then, on a list of the made-up words, you are asked to write the matching real words. The twenty slides are shown a second and third time, each time in a different order. The underlying memory is being thought of as a language-learning aptitude, helpful in learning a new language, unfamiliar terms, and technical jargon.

Do you have rhythm? The sense of rhythm is marked by the emphasis of time or loudness, or both. It is not limited to the sense of hearing, though it is measured in that manner. A strong sense of rhythm with a memory for intricate patterns can be observed in the performance of a drummer. Poetry has rhythm. Certain kinds of work and recreation offer outlets for your rhythm memory.

Differing degrees of physical energy and agility are exerted on the various musical instruments, and conducting can be made, by some, into an exhausting job. Beyond physical energy, the piano makes use of a kind of muscle memory that enables the performer to reach out the precise distance, without looking, to hit the correct keys on the piano keyboard. The same ability helps you to touch the tip of your nose with your eyes closed. Performers on some of the other instruments, to some extent, use the same kind of memory. But as an aptitude, this type of memory has not yet been measured, not even by an experimental test.

Singers carry their musical instruments with them at all times, together with an almost fanatical, subjective devotion to perfection, arrived at through endless practice and careful attention to the physical maintenance of their instruments. Choral singing, on the other hand, does not demand that the practice or physical maintenance of the voice be as intense, but it substantially increases the importance of rhythm. The singer has no need for dexterity of fingers except in the case of self accompaniment. Ideaphoria invigorates the singer's performance and motivates the learning and possibly the writing of new songs.

If you are in accounting, or selling, or advertising and if you have the musical aptitudes, you might prefer to do your work with an organization that is in some way related to music. Even if you are a high school dropout and can find no better beginning job than work as a janitor, you would be better off working for a factory or store that handles musical merchandise, for example, than for some insurance company.

The differing ages of maturity of the various aptitudes complicate the problem of choosing a career. The precocious musical child is usually encouraged to be a professional musician. After several years of musical training, the artistic aptitudes may become prominent and their use may divert attention away from music. As each later maturing aptitude appears, it tends to motivate the musical child in a new direction.

One girl at age 15 did not make a single error on the test for tonal memory and scored high in both rhythm memory and pitch discrimination. If she had applied for admission at a school of music where enrollment is open only to those who score high in the music tests, she would have been classified as a "safe" student, one of the group most likely to succeed.

Distraction from her music was experienced before the time of testing. She had been drawing dress designs, an activity that used her structural visualization, artistic aptitudes, and imagination. Her aptitude inventory and accompanying discussion resulted in a decision to combine all of her aptitudes and interests in costume and set designing in the field of television.

An architecture student who felt the need for an aptitude inventory made almost a perfect score on the music tests. After being in school bands for seven years and having a dance band of his own during high school, his structural visualization and artistic aptitudes had pulled him into architecture. Still tied to music, he wanted to decide which way to go. He finally decided to continue in architecture, followed by graduate work in city and regional planning with an emphasis on acoustical engineering, which would have used his musical aptitudes

A third example illustrates the influence of inductive reasoning on the career choice of a musically talented person. A particular young woman, a freshman in college, had performed solo work and had been active in vocal and instrumental groups. She scored at the 95th percentile on the English vocabulary test and was familiar with most of the items on a music vocabulary test. Her inductive reasoning and excellent vocabulary were probably what had motivated her interest in writing during her senior year in high school. Her decision to prepare for a career as a music critic and writer in the musical world seemed to be a suitable choice that would allow her to use all of her aptitudes.

Deciding to be an engineer, or a salesman, or a physician on the basis of a single test can be as risky as a decision to be a musician on the basis of just the music tests. Only a complete inventory of your aptitudes will determine whether you have the helpful supplementary aptitudes or the unneeded distracting ones.

A memory for tunes may attract you to music and possibly to musical performance, but if you score low in pitch discrimination, you'll spare the ears of those who are sensitive to pitch by avoiding the study of the violin or voice. A fixed-pitch keyboard instrument is the one for you, but still other factors may play a part here. Slowness in perceptual speed will limit your sight reading where the music is written on two or more clefs. Of course, you'll not need to read at sight if you can memorize the music as Toscanini did when conducting symphony orchestras.

Slowness in dexterity may limit you to the amateur ranks, but go ahead and play some anyway if you have the urge. You can learn in a do-it-yourself way or by taking private lessons or, as some are doing, you may enroll in a class for amateurs offered at many schools.

Chapter 12 / WAYS WITH WORDS

You are fortunate that your vocabulary does not enter the world with you as the natural mental factors do. The learnable feature of vocabulary allows you to design and build this important part of your intellectual structure to your own specifications.

Vocabulary may not be a natural trait but there is a natural way to learn it. Observe how a child learns the meanings of words. First he hears a word spoken in sentences. He may try to say the word without knowing the meaning. Sooner or later he tries to put the word in a phrase or sentence, but with the wrong meaning. A parent sets him straight.

The same learning process continues as the child grows older and attends school where teachers and schoolmates perform the corrective function of pointing out the proper meaning. The process begins to fail when school and family are left behind, when there are no parents or teachers to assist in the final step of learning. At the adult stage you need to correct your own words. Review the process: first you hear a word several times; next you try to use it; finally you establish the exact meaning. The natural process of learning words takes place most effectively when parents, teachers, and ultimately you appreciate the value of a comprehensive vocabulary.

When it comes to reading, you are responsible from the very beginning for learning the correct meaning of new words. Your teacher and classmates cannot assist you with a newly read word unless you happen to try it out on them. You must be your own teacher. In some cases you will want to consult a dictionary when you first come across a new word. The more common and more efficient way is to look it up after you have seen it several times in different sentences.

The words of the English language (or any language) can be arranged in a graduated order of difficulty, ranging from the very easiest words learned by toddlers to the most difficult words known by very few. Every word in the language appears to have its own place in the order of difficulty, a sequence the same in Massachusetts, California, Pennsylvania, Texas, Illinois, Oklahoma, New York, and other locations where testing and research have taken place. The position in the sequence is not dependent on teachers or textbooks, politicians or parents. Rather, it is somehow inherent in each word itself—probably in the idea that it conveys. A word's degree of difficulty does not necessarily correspond with its length or its frequency of use.

Words, which symbolize ideas, usually are learned in order, first the easier, then the progressively harder ones. Along the scale of increasing difficulty you will know almost all of the words up to a certain point, which might be called your "borderline, or frontier, of knowledge." It is the words just beyond this borderline—words you have seen, heard spoken, or tried to use—that you can learn most efficiently. Your frontier will advance as you refine the meaning of these words, one by one. Learning becomes more difficult when you skip the frontier words and try to learn a word you've never seen before. The order-of-difficulty concept is implicit in the metaphor of vocabulary *building*. You don't want to work on fifth-story words before the foundation has even been finished.

This approach to vocabulary learning is the result of the Foundation's consideration of the basic question: what is the most effective way to teach a student vocabulary? There are, of course, many different ways. One is to teach students the parts of the words— roots, prefixes, and suffixes—thus giving them the tools to work out the meanings of words on their own. Another approach is to teach words used in a particular subject. Still another approach is to drill on words that are considered to be important for some reason—for example, words that have appeared on the College Board tests.

All of these approaches have advantages and disadvantages. Their basic disadvantage is that they tend to ignore both the individual student's level of word knowledge, and the range of difficulty of individual words (even words that concern the same subject or have similar roots). For example, *presumptuous* might be taught to a student who doesn't know what confident means, *isthmus* to someone who only vaguely understands what a *continent* is. This is often a waste of time. Students might be able to memorize a definition or synonym of a difficult word, and get it right on a test, but if the word is too far removed from their experience or understanding they are not likely to make it a permanent part of their vocabulary.

We feel that the best approach is to select words that are at the individual student's level of knowledge—words the student is familiar with but not quite sure of, words the student doesn't know but which represent concepts he or she is capable of grasping, words the student is ready to learn.

The Foundation's method does two things: first, through a vocabulary test it determines a student's level on a vocabulary scale. Second, it orders words by finding the average vocabulary level of students who are at the point of achieving a precise knowledge of each word. The word *decay* is known by three-fourths of students scoring at the low end of the vocabulary scale (51 on a scale from 40 to 225), so it is an easy word. *Connote* is known to three-fourths of students scoring 176; it is a hard word. *Alliance*, known to three-fourths of students scoring 111, is intermediate in difficulty.

Thus, students are matched with words at their level of understanding. Studying these words should be easier and more profitable than attempting to learn words that are far beyond this level. Words at this level that a student doesn't know should be relatively easy to learn, since the student is capable of understanding words of similar difficulty.

Building your vocabulary by following these principles of learning is made easy by the use of the Johnson O'Connor Research Foundation's eight *Wordbooks*, in which 1,440 words—180 per *Wordbook*—are discussed in order of difficulty, ranging from words known to children nine years old to words unknown to 99 percent of adults.

In contrast to the natural intellectual factors that rise to a plateau before gradually declining, vocabulary rises rapidly during the early years, then more slowly, but it need never reach a plateau or decline. As a result, the process of learning words by sharpening the concept

41

of slightly familiar terms applies not only to children but to adults. When you are young, the world judges you on your potential. As you go through your twenties, thirties, and forties, the world looks more and more at how much you know and what you can do.

Aptitudes will give you a good start but it takes vocabulary to keep you going. Don't wait too long to start working with words.

Four general types of errors take place at the frontier of a person's knowledge of words:
1. Confusion of words that sound or look alike.
2. Confusion of terms in the same situation.
3. Lack of precision in meaning.
4. Confusion of a word with its opposite.

The four types of errors correspond roughly to the four stages of learning new words, as judged by relative positions of occurrence in vocabulary tests where the words are arranged in a graduated order of difficulty. When incorrectly marked choices are studied, beginning at the end of vocabulary tests where no words are known, we see the results of sheer guessing.

Moving gradually away from the hardest words, the first type of error is the confusion of words that look alike or sound alike: fiesta, siesta; shrill, chill; coup, scoop; defied, deified.

The second type of error is the confusion of terms in the same situation or classification: is a benediction an offering or a blessing? Is a prognosis a prediction or a prescription?

Moving toward easier words, there is a lack of precision in meanings: a private door is labeled to keep out unwanted visitors, a secret door is never labeled. Shouting means loud voices, not fighting.

In the fourth type of error, words are confused with their opposites: Luminous means bright, not dim. Does anterior mean front or back?

The sequential nature of the steps in the learning process applies also to specialized bodies of knowledge. Furthermore, the extent of a person's specialized vocabulary, such as that of physics, appears to be related to the size of his or her English vocabulary. Delving into specialized subject matter areas bring additional general terms into one's vocabulary. The word stress, for example, is fully understood only after its literal meaning is learned. In this way, the learning of general vocabulary and specialized vocabularies are interdependent. A lagging behind in the growth of one becomes a limiting factor in the maximum growth of the other. The enlargement of your general body of knowledge by the contribution of terms from specialized fields takes place at a maximum rate in a formal educational setting.

Grades in school are not important to some but they may be to you if you are a student. Consciously enlarging your vocabulary will almost guarantee higher grades for you. Reports of individuals who have followed a vocabulary-building program, as well as studies of grades made by students at different vocabulary levels, show the value of word knowledge. Similar vocabulary levels make for compatibility among fellow workers, friends, and family. An engineer who grew up in New England was working in another part of the country where he always felt out of place. On learning that his vocabulary level was far above his fellow workers, he realized that he was working in the wrong part of the country.

Companies have different vocabulary levels, too, even in the same part of the country. Executive branches of government, from local to national, can vary from term to term in their vocabulary levels. The top members of an organization set the pace. A low vocabulary head usually surrounds himself with compatible assistants. When appointments are made from unknown applicants, the low-vocabulary person doing the hiring will be inclined to hire a person with whom he feels comfortable.

Schools have different vocabulary levels, not to mention the wide range within a single classroom. The generation gap is partly a vocabulary gap. Variations in vocabulary level occur among sororities, fraternities, and probably among social groups, ethnic groups, and religious denominations. Suggestions have been made that communities and even nations have different vocabulary levels, compounding the problem of communication when the two nations speak in different tongues.

The evidence that general and specialized learning proceed hand in hand, that each one enhances the other, could lead parents and teachers to maximize a child's potential in life by exposure to a great variety of specialized areas. The individual child's aptitude pattern might influence a concentration in some directions, but the wide exposure could extend through high school and possibly longer. A general education of this type would be broader, more comprehensive and relevant than the limited, classical type.

Money is not important to some people but it may be to you. As with grades in school, money earnings are related to vocabulary. Within each occupation, those with larger vocabularies are more likely to profit. Put a dollar sign in front of each additional word you learn.

It is interesting to note here that company executives scored higher in the vocabulary test than any other selected group with which the Foundation has experimented—and this result was totally unforeseen. Was this luck? Or was it significant of something not recognized? The Foundation listed the vocabulary scores of one hundred executives and, parallel with them, the scores of one hundred miscellaneous college graduates. The difference between the two arrays was striking. Only nine percent of the college graduates scored as high as the average executive.

Why do large vocabularies characterize executives and possibly outstanding men and women in other fields? The final answer seems to be that words are the instruments by means of which men and women grasp the thoughts of others and with which they do much of their own thinking. They are the tools of thought.

Do you aspire to great accomplishments not measured in dollars? Here again a mastery of words will increase your prospects. Do you wish to think more clearly and comprehensively? The response is the same; we think with words. Can you express your feelings verbally? Are you effective in putting across your ideas? Do you need self-confidence? Would you have people respect you? Would you like to compensate for an aptitude that you don't have? Do you want to lift yourself by your own bootstraps?

You may be wondering if vocabulary merits this kind of praise. Isn't there some disadvantage to a large vocabulary? Yes, it can be misused. Showing off by using difficult words is one abuse, but you'll find the same among those with smaller vocabularies. A large vocabulary is more than knowing the difficult words; it is knowing the easier words more thoroughly and using them with greater precision. Vocabularies can be compared to automobiles. An eight-cylinder car operates more smoothly at low speeds than one with four cylinders. A powerful vocabulary gives you the facility to use the easier words more smoothly.

To summarize. You have decided to enlarge your vocabulary. How do you go about it? If you wish, you may pick out a strange word and with some effort learn its meaning. New words are being thrust in front of you constantly, demanding to be learned. But learning a strange, new word is very much like learning to know a person you've met for the first time. You become acquainted by degrees, learning a little more with each meeting. The efficient way, and the natural way from childhood on, is to straighten out one by one the meaning of words that already are slightly familiar to you, your vocabulary frontier words, your borderline words. Pick out a word you have seen or heard, possibly one you have tried to use. Learn its precise meaning. You will remember it easily. Then pick another word. You will be doing deliberately what comes naturally.

Chapter 13 / FRAGMENTATION OF KNOWLEDGE

Speculation on the nature of human beings was centered in philosophy and theology until the sixteenth and seventeenth centuries when the scientific era of medicine began, ushered in by the English physician, William Harvey, who discovered the circulation of blood. Specialization came as the increasing amount of medical knowledge grew too large for any one person to comprehend. Chemistry, biology, physiology, and other physical sciences made discoveries to explain the workings of the human body.

In their study of the physical parts of humans not explained by the earlier thinkers, the physicians and scientists tended to disregard the nonphysical aspects of human life. Psychiatrists in the field of medicine began to correct the imbalance by relating the emotions to unusual behavior.

As in medicine and in each of the sciences, the increasing amount of knowledge in psychology has resulted in more than thirty areas of specialization. One of these, the study of intellectual factors, has produced still more explanations of human behavior. The progression in the scientific study of humans from physical to emotional to intellectual roughly parallels the progression in evolutionary development.

It is natural that the specialists in each area of each science believe that their particular language best explains the nature of man. Because of the very fact of their concentration, the specialty groups find it difficult, if not impossible, to interpret human behavior in any language but their own. As a result, very few attempts are made to integrate the vast amount of accumulated knowledge about humans.

You, as a layman, must try to do this if you are to benefit from what is known. The task is difficult.

When the number of human variables becomes too large, when things become too complicated to understand, one is almost forced to resort to some simple explanation, to a capsule description. We'll describe a friend's behavior as brilliant or stupid. In the classroom we'll say that a certain girl is a troublemaker. We'll call a boy hyperactive and give him drugs to alter his behavior without bothering to learn if he is suffering from lead poisoning, or poor nutrition, or an unsettled home life, or an unchallenged imagination.

The explosion of knowledge has resulted in its fragmentation. Roger J. Williams, the distinguished biochemist at the University of Texas, has written a book called *The Human Frontier* in which he pleads eloquently for the development of a new branch of applied science, the science of "Humanics," which would undertake a comprehensive study of individual human beings. He contends that the investigation of man has fallen into the hands of specialists, each working within a narrow field. He believes that a new type of specialist is needed—one who will coordinate the findings of all the specialists in the study of the individual.

In his later book, *You are Extraordinary*, Williams emphasizes how each person is unique and highly distinctive in not several but in hundreds of ways (both physical and mental, if you feel the need to make the separation). He shows how one area of knowledge can throw light on the problems in another. He illustrates the normal variations in muscles. The so-called minor pectoralis muscle is attached to the ribs differently in each person. The variety of attachments causes each of us to draw our shoulders downward and forward in a singular manner. Watch baseball pitchers and you will see that each one makes this and other motions in a characteristic way.

Another illustration shows six different arrangements of one specific muscle on the back of the hand, the muscle which shortens when you point with your index finger. The pattern of attachment on two of the hands in the illustration would cause the index finger and the adjacent finger to move together. Every hand is distinctive not only in respect to this one muscle but in its entire structure. Williams tells of Robert Schumann, the composer, who suffered exasperation for years because he didn't know about the difference in hands. He had strong musical leanings, composed music when he was a child, and had access to the best teachers. He also had motivation, determination, and persistence, practicing as much as seven hours a day, but he failed dismally in his highest ambition to become the leading piano virtuoso of his time. He had continued difficulty with some of the fingers of his right hand. He worked on the problem, using all sorts of methods to strengthen and train his fingers. One device suspended his fourth finger in a sling while he practiced with the others. Some reports indicate that he injured his hand in the attempt to make it behave. He eventually gave up the idea of concert work and devoted himself to composition.

Williams would have the integrated knowledge from all of the specialists applied to individual humans but, by his examples, indicates the need for doing it one step at a time. He suggests that those in each field try to build bridges to other islands of knowledge.

The bridge of biochemistry links two physical sciences, resulting in the benefit of better nutrition, which in turn benefits emotional and intellectual functioning. Studies of intellectual abilities have built bridges to education, to industry, and now to social and family life. More exploration and bridge building lie ahead, some of which you can do with your newly acquired knowledge of aptitudes.

There is abundant evidence that on our arrival as newborn babies, each of us brings along a host of individual characteristics. In the years since our arrival, we have accumulated many layers of cultural polish and have nursed the bruises of environmental impacts.

You can better understand the nature of what came with you and the influence of the experiences since your birth by a study of what the many specialists have learned. But don't let them subdivide you. The parts carved out by the sciences are for study and descriptive purposes only. You are a single, functioning person, with the various functions interrelated, each one dependent on all of the others.

Chapter 14 / INTERESTS AND APTITUDES

What interests you? Do a large number of things attract you, or just a few? How many times have your interests changed since you were five or six? Do your interests agree with your aptitudes? You are fortunate if they do.

An interest based on your aptitudes is not a passing interest except in one of several situations. An ability that matures later in one's development may usurp the dominant place of the earlier ability, as in the case when music is the early interest. A needed helping aptitude may not be present. Lack of dexterity with small tools, for example, may discourage the boy who is attracted to dentistry, or having artistic interests may lead a student into architecture where the going is rough without the ability to visualize in three dimensions. A person may have too many aptitudes to allow more than a passing interest in a single area, or a vivid imagination may create an interest in most everything.

A child's interests widen gradually. To his mother's comment that "Mark likes everybody," a four-year-old boy startled his mother and her guests by responding, "No, I don't." His eyes sparkled with delight as he quickly added, "I don't know everybody." Interests are like that. You can't have an interest in something until you know about it.

In earlier years, a child's interests are dependent on his or her immediate surroundings. These interests—in a favorite toy, for example, or a kind of play, or a reaction to food—can all be expressed without words. Later, words are needed to express interests—as in the desire, for example, to become a pilot or a ballerina. As interests develop and change in the expanding world of a child, conflicts may emerge between internal interests and the influence of external forces, such as parents and society. A child who grows up in a seaport or in a farming community may develop an interest in the familiar. On the other hand, he or she may develop a negative reaction to it. As with the growth of vocabulary, there is a broadening in the spectrum of interests if the child is exposed to a great variety of specialized areas.

The informal use of interests through the years as a basis of vocational choice has been supplemented more recently by the use of standardized tests. The interest test-makers, in formalizing the assessment of interests, gained statistical exactness by testing large numbers of individuals. But in the process, they lost touch in the application of the data to the individual, because anything made for mass consumption is tailored, necessarily, to the average person.

Interest tests do not answer as many questions for you as aptitude tests do, but they are widely used because of their economy in costs of materials and the small amount of time and skill needed for the administration and interpretation. They can be self-administered in large groups, and the interpretive, computerized printouts can be understood by the student without any professional assistance.

Interest tests were developed in one of two ways. E. K. Strong determined the interests of physicians, accountants, salesmen, and a number of other occupational groups. Physicians, for example, might be interested in helping people, playing golf, and attending concerts. Let's say the chief interests of the accountant group are in reading, opera, and gardening. The interests of salesmen may lie in baseball, bridge, and jazz. The interests of each of Strong's occupational groups were then formulated into a scale for that occupation.

The examinee's interests are indicated on a master list that is matched against each of the occupational scales. In the end, you'll have interests in common with physicians if you like to help people, play golf, and attend concerts. Different interests will put you in the accounting or in the sales group.

In the development of his Vocational Preference Record, G. F. Kuder started with various kinds of general activities, such as outdoor, scientific, computational, and persuasive, some of which might apply to more than one occupation, or combine into a single occupation. An examinee's pattern of scores in the different areas is compared with the pattern found in various occupations. Kuder later designed an Occupational Interest Survey in which the examinee's interests are compared directly with different occupations. Designers of interest tests make two questionable assumptions: one, that all people have the same number of interests; and, the other, that you cannot have an equal amount of interest in two different things.

You can make a systematic but personal appraisal of your own interests by constructing a short inventory that will allow you to indicate equal degrees of interest in any number of areas. List a number of occupations and rate yourself opposite each item by assigning a number from one to five to express your degree of interest. In the process of choosing a career, select for initial investigation several of the occupations that received the highest ratings. Analyze each one in terms of how your own aptitudes would be helpful in doing the work of that occupation. Are there any aptitudes left over that are apparently not of any use? Look for some specialty in the occupation that might use the ones left over.

Of course, one's mental image of each occupation has been formed by observing, hearing, reading, or watching television. Is police work accurately portrayed in most television shows? How about architecture, or accounting, or management? Indeed, one's mental image may vary widely from the actual work. Research in such books as the *Occupational Outlook Handbook* may provide more accurate clues, as will visits to the workplace and interviews with people there. In addition, there are literally thousands of occupation-specific periodicals that offer a wealth of information about every imaginable field.

When looking for career information, it may also help to remember that few people begin at the top. Do beginners in the same occupation do a different kind of work, using a different set of aptitudes? Engineering uses your head, but many entry jobs in engineering firms are essentially clerical in nature. A person scoring low in Graphoria may find it helpful to keep in mind that entry-level "paper-pushing" tasks may not be the ultimate nature of the job. Just be ready for it, and prepare for the most advanced positions where you can use a greater number of aptitudes.

Your first job was working as a student, so whatever occupation you have chosen to follow is not your first one. Because few occupations call for the scholarly activities demanded in formal education, you may find that the aptitudes helpful in your chosen occupation are not the same aptitudes you relied on in your job as a student.

Chapter 15 / DIVERSITY OF APTITUDES WITHIN A SINGLE OCCUPATION

If you haven't become convinced by now that all the jobs in one occupation are not alike, perhaps the ensuing discussion will clinch the point. The picturing of an occupational group in terms of a generalized job description or aptitude pattern does not describe every task or every person in the occupation, only the majority. Mathematically, it would be impossible for all members of each occupational group to be alike in aptitude patterns. There are more than five million possible pattern combinations, when you consider the low scores as well as the high scores of nineteen human variables, and there are fewer than thirty thousand kinds of jobs.

Occupational titles are misleading anyway. They are but classifications made for the sake of convenience. No two life-insurance salesmen sell in the same fashion. The work of a chemist in pure research is not identical to the chemist's work in manufacturing. Even two people working at the same assigned duties in the same organization will approach their work differently.

When you look at occupations, what at first may appear as a narrow field of work may prove to be, on careful scrutiny, a broad area with subdivisions and highly specialized jobs within it. A good example is geology, one division of which is petroleum geology.

The writer of the present volume prepared an article on the aptitude patterns of petroleum geologists for the Tulsa Geological Society Digest in 1954. Portions of the article constitute the remainder of this chapter.

Fortunately for those who enter it, petroleum geology has so many facets that a geologist with almost any kind of aptitude pattern can find a suitable type of work, providing he knows what is best. Petroleum geology, already experienced in utilizing as fully as possible its physical resources, has begun to make a fuller use of its human resources through a careful use of aptitude analysis. It's a case of the square peg being shown the square hole into which he can fit, not by hunch or guess or chance, but through an objective, scientific measurement of his different kinds of memories, dexterities, and visualization.

The delving into the recesses of the human mind during the last half century has resulted in several discoveries, the first being that mental ability is not a single entity. Instead, it is composed of separate and distinct parts, each part being an independent element. Tests show that each person has a number of these elements, or aptitudes, the combination being known as the person's aptitude pattern. Furthermore, each occupational field, such as geology, tends to attract people with similar but not identical aptitude patterns.

The second significant discovery in the history of aptitude testing was that some of the mental traits appeared to pass from one generation to the next, in the same manner as physical traits.

The third important discovery was that idle aptitudes cause more trouble than those you lack. The work of a bookkeeper may suffer from an excessive flow of ideas that keeps his mind a hundred miles away. He may be more unhappy and inefficient than the man who is slower but whose normal flow of ideas permits him to be more contented with his work.

The straightforward analysis of the mental traits of an individual in a manner similar to engineering practice has appealed to scientific-thinking industries and business. The four earliest branches of the Johnson O'Connor Research Foundation, in Boston, New York, Philadelphia, and Chicago, tested employees and established characteristic aptitude patterns in heavy steel, textile and other industries found in those parts of the country. Later, branches were opened in Los Angeles, Tulsa, Fort Worth and Baytown, Texas. Information has been accumulated on vegetable oil producers, electric utility company workers, aluminum manufacturers, and others. Around 100 petroleum geologists from one company alone have been assayed to date in addition to more than another hundred members of various companies in the petroleum industry whose jobs range from roughneck to refinery superintendent and company president. Of importance to the next generation, the knowledge provides assistance in the planning of careers.

Finger dexterity is the most frequently found aptitude in petroleum geologists. It is the aptitude that helps them to handle things quickly and easily with their fingers. The fumbling high school chemistry student who is all thumbs is not attracted to further laboratory courses and so usually does not enter geology. He becomes another example of the survival of the fittest.

Tweezer dexterity is the ability to handle small tools and instruments. Sometimes mistaken in childhood for engineering ability, it does help in geology when accompanied by some of the other useful aptitudes. It is separate and distinct from finger dexterity. Memory for design helps the geologist to remember maps, drawings, logs, and formations.

Structural visualization, the engineering aptitude, helps in structural geology and in all other situations where it is desirable to picture mentally any three-dimensional concept. One University of Texas student, realizing his handicap of not having this particular aptitude, deliberately avoided the Gulf coast area when seeking a position, knowing that in other areas he would encounter fewer geologic faults to visualize.

Inductive reasoning is the ability to go from the particular to the general and draw inferences. Coupled with ideaphoria and objective personality, it is an aid to employee training and other types of group-influencing activities. Coupled with structural visualization, it aids in exploration work. With structural visualization and subjective personality it becomes a research tool, helping to correlate seemingly unrelated data. With ideaphoria it helps in writing concise and pointed reports and letters.

Inductive reasoning begins to decline in the twenties, only a few years after it reaches maturity. The older geologist learns to depend on increasing knowledge and experience. The recognition of this double difference between young and old helps to explain the conflict so often occurring in a group discussion. Actually, each age group has something valuable to contribute toward a group effort. Several companies are beginning to capitalize on this. One company is forming a "junior" board composed entirely of young employees with

55

inductive reasoning into whose laps will be tossed a problem together with a full background of facts. The conclusions are then to be returned to the older group for deliberate consideration. In some cases, a young man acts as an executive assistant. In still others, interplay of young aptitudes and mature knowledge is less formal.

Tonal memory, the memory for musical tunes, is the aptitude that points toward activity in music. When coupled with structural visualization it often leads an engineer into electrical or acoustical fields. In geology, geophysics offers a compatible environment for this aptitude pattern.

As with most other occupations, there is in geology a variety of jobs suitable for both subjective and objective persons. The subjective person is happier and more successful when doing work of an individual nature. The subjective geologist prefers to work on projects of his own where his success depends on his own efforts rather than on what he can get others to do. The objective person does better working with and through others. Subjective geologists excel in research; objective geologists in all kinds of contact work, in supervisory positions, and in jobs where the work resembles selling.

A rapid flow of ideas is found to be useful in geology wherever a large amount of talking to other people takes place, such as in sales work. One large oil company chose one of its objective geologists with ideaphoria to represent their interests before the Texas Railroad Commission, the regulatory agency that controls the amount of production from each well.

The most difficult problem, both to the man himself and to his company, is having more aptitudes than any single kind of work can use. Whenever he tries to settle down in a job that uses only a few of his aptitudes, the other aptitudes clamor for action, like a gang of evil genies. He changes jobs in an effort to use the idle aptitudes. Now others become idle and frustrating. Or, if circumstances force him to stay in one job, he may take up a dozen hobbies. One satisfactory adjustment is for him to work in a small company where his job will be many-sided, thereby using first one aptitude and then another. Several geologists of this type have become either independent operators or consultants. One small company has put a too-many-aptitude geologist in charge of a three man "task force" that goes from one place to another, doing highly varied jobs.

Graphoria, the accounting aptitude, so-called because of its importance to that profession, is the natural speed and accuracy that enables one to sight-read piano music rapidly, or to make easy work of a mass of tabulations and calculations on paper. It helps in the administrative, clerical, and financial jobs in geology.

One geologist with an aptitude pattern not at all similar to most geologists, but who had advanced to a position of authority in his company, admitted that he had entered geology because of its glamour and not because of any particular bent. He had coasted through high school on his graphoria (he scored at the 99th percentile) and his superior English vocabulary (ten years advanced). Experiencing no weak spots in his education, he thought that he could succeed at anything he tried. In geology he found success but, unfortunately, not happiness.

Three discoveries in the history of aptitude testing have been noted: the independence of aptitudes, the inheritance of aptitudes, and the distraction of idle aptitudes. The fourth, and by far the most important discovery in the history of aptitude testing is that aptitudes alone will never make you successful. About all that a full and proper use of your aptitudes can do is to increase somewhat your chances for a satisfying life. Knowledge and only knowledge, coupled with your aptitudes, will make you successful.

You may have aptitudes helpful in geology. You may have a desire to become a geologist. But you won't reach that goal until after you have gained a lot of knowledge about your chosen field. This kind of specialized knowledge is thought by many to be sufficient, but additional general knowledge, indicated by the extent of your English vocabulary, seems to be the kind that more often leads to worldly success. One geologist summed it up in this way: aptitudes for happiness, knowledge for success.

Chapter 16 / WHERE CAN YOU USE YOUR APTITUDES?

Your selection of a career is not a one-shot decision to be made when a specified birthday arrives. It is such a long-term process that many are referring to it as career development, beginning back in your childhood with all of its influences, and extending forward into the working years of your life as you make advancements and adjustments.

You have had an inventory of your aptitudes and knowledge, with an explanation of your scores on the different tests. You discussed your career potentials and possibly other implications of your measured abilities. You may want to return at some later date for a follow-up appointment to check your improvement in vocabulary and try some of the newer, experimental tests, but for now the testing is over and you are on your own.

If you are like most people, you will begin to translate human activities into the language of aptitudes. You'll say to a friend, "Oh, I see that you are using your ideaphoria today." A systematic use of this kind of thinking will enable you to learn that there are quite a few places where you can use your aptitudes effectively.

You will find in this chapter information on a small number of occupational areas, followed by information on a wide variety of more specific careers. Both sections are arranged alphabetically. The latter section includes detailed information on job descriptions and educational requirements, as well as listings of required or recommended college subjects.

The following discussion of accordion playing will illustrate how you can analyze any occupation in terms of aptitudes. You will have a chance to try your hand at doing the same thing with the work of accounting, and you can gain additional practice with other occupations.

Among the hundreds of musicians who have taken aptitude tests, the number of accordion players is too small to give a statistical picture of this occupational group. However, enough is known of the nature of aptitudes and of the nature of performers on other musical instruments to permit a fairly accurate estimate of the aptitudes helpful in accordion playing.

Tonal memory not only enables music performers to recognize and memorize the melodic movements in music but undoubtedly is the principal motivating factor that first attracts them to music. As with people who cannot forget numbers easily, those with tonal memory find that tunes stick in their heads without any effort. Accordion performers play from memory, but their need to read music from the printed page when learning new and intricate numbers makes graphoria a valuable aid.

Aptitudes contributing to your success in a given job can be rated as to the degree of helpfulness. Tonal memory probably would be rated the highest for accordion playing. You could adjust or compensate for the absence of any of the others. Slow fingers would limit you to slow numbers. A knowledge of harmonic progressions and the learning of a tune by listening would compensate for slowness in reading music.

Does your acquaintance with the work done by accountants extend beyond the vague impression that they keep written records of business transactions? You can supplement the brief job descriptions in this chapter by reading, visiting places of work, and asking questions.

Do you remember the principles to follow in making a vocational decision, whether it is your first job, or a promotion, or a transfer to a different kind of work? First, you learn about the kind of work to be performed. Then you consider your aptitudes, either singly or in combination, to see if they would be useful in doing the work.

With your understanding of aptitudes, which one do you think would be of greatest help to you in accounting? Yes, you are correct! It's graphoria. Nobody could miss that one. Would any of your other aptitudes help you in keeping records? Would a subjective person be more satisfied with this kind of work? Do you have any other aptitude that could be used in a particular kind of record-keeping for a business handling a certain kind of product? Do you have an aptitude that might be a distracting factor? Easy, isn't it, to evaluate a job when you know what kind of work it involves? Just follow the same procedure in analyzing each of the following occupations or any additional ones not included.

The universality of record-keeping in educational, military, and industrial settings has produced hundreds of research studies from many sources dealing with the aptitude for doing paper and pencil work. The ability to predict success by means of a simple, number comparison test led to the hiring of clerical workers on the basis of their test performance.

The industrial practice, still followed by some, of using a single test in hiring for a given job, was extended to the use of dexterity tests in hiring for assembly work and mechanical knowledge tests in hiring for mechanical jobs. The practice of relying on a single aptitude test, at least in the early days, probably resulted from honest ignorance of the multiple needs of some occupations, or of the distracting effect of idle aptitudes.

Occasional requests from employees for permission to transfer from one department of a company to another, with the accompanying need to take an additional test, gradually pointed to the advantage of asking each new employee to take several tests. This permitted a comparison of one occupational group with another, but hiring in most situations continued to be a process of picking a person for the job.

From the very first, the General Electric Company tested employees only after they had been hired. The plant was so large and the jobs were so varied that a person could find some place in the organization to use most any combination of aptitudes. From the first, each tested employee was informed of the results and their meaning, enabling the individual to share with the company the responsibility of planning ahead for the most satisfying kind of work. This type of testing resulted in finding a job for the person, rather than a person for the job.

Smaller organizations cannot follow the same practice, but the results of an aptitude inventory, interpreted to a rejected applicant, will give an individual the permanent benefit of increased self-knowledge.

Sometimes it is better to promote an employee than to fire him. A manufacturer of machine tools in Chicago was about to discharge a clerk in the bookkeeping department. The man was capable but his heart was not in his work and he no longer was earning his keep. When tested, the man showed aptitude for accounting but he scored equally high in aptitude for engineering. He had been doing straight bookkeeping, juggling groups and columns of figures. Instead of finding himself out of a job, the man found himself in a higher paying job in the cost accounting department where he was brought into contact with blueprints, graphs, and tools, almost like being in an engineering office. Here he not only was able to use, but was required to use his structural visualization, along with the other ability he had thought he hated.

AGRICULTURE

The work done in farm-related businesses varies greatly but mostly involves contact work with people. Aptitudes useful to sales and management in other fields are useful in performing the same functions in the agricultural field.

Credit managers and appraisers work for financial institutions who loan money for land, farm equipment, and livestock. Buyers of produce will contract to buy farm products for markets and food processing plants. One outgoing, friendly sort of man spends all of his time visiting producers of potatoes in an effort to persuade them to sell their crops to his employer, a large potato chip company.

The sales and manufacture of supplies, feeds, and equipment use a variety of aptitudes. Agricultural engineers, in addition to designing tractors, soil-conditioning equipment, and harvesters, provide assistance to food producers in problems of irrigation, drainage, and flood control.

A desire on your part to enter this wide field should lead you to investigate each area of concentration thoroughly.

Agriculture production itself is big business, both in livestock and crops. By the use of expensive, labor-saving machinery, family farms and ranches are becoming bigger. Professional managers operate a number of large acreages owned by corporations. Agriculture production on a family unit is a many-aptitude job. When production units increase in size, the multi-faceted duties of the small operation became divided and subdivided in the same manner as in urban factories that start small and grow large, resulting in the use of fewer aptitudes in each specialized job.

With all kinds of people doing all sorts of work in agriculture, you will be able to use almost any combination of abilities.

Special knowledge and skills make possible the efficient production of each kind of crop and livestock. Experience with the midwestern crops of wheat, oats, soybeans, and corn isn't of much value in the production of sugarcane, rice, cotton, or cranberries. Citrus, vegetable crops, and viticulture, the growing of grapes, require still different techniques. The specialty of apiculture, the raising and care of bees, is of value both for the food crop of honey and for the pollination of blossoms in orchard and field crops. Knowledge of genetics produces better strains of plants and animals, and soil chemistry contributes to more nutritious foods.

Other divisions of agriculture include nonedible crops: tobacco, ornamental plants, trees, flower and vegetable seeds. One company in California, has made a specialty of processing tons of tomatoes each year for the seeds alone, which are sold to commercial growers.

ANTHROPOLOGY

Cultural anthropologists trace the origin and evolutionary development of humans through the study of customs, traditions, religions, and languages. Physical anthropologists are concerned primarily with the biology of human groups, studying the evolutionary changes and geographical distribution of physical characteristics and material possessions.

Ecologists will study the relation between man and his environment. Those studying ethnology are interested in living people, usually primitive communities, their customs, and beliefs. Some anthropologists prefer to specialize in archaeology, the study of ancient peoples, often in field work and by excavation of relics and artifacts. Anthropologists gain satisfaction in knowing that their work helps to create a better life for everyone through a better understanding of humanity, past and present.

Do you think that structural visualization would be useful in physical anthropology? Could you find a use for inductive reasoning in research? What other aptitudes would find an outlet in this scientific field? Can you see any place in anthropology for an objective person? Keep on asking questions like these when you are investigating the suitability of any occupation.

ART

Dexterity with the fingers helps in modeling with clay, while dexterity with tools comes into the picture when carving wood or stone. If you'll be on the lookout for it, you will notice that the work of the occasional painter with structural visualization shows a three-dimensional quality.

Each medium of artistic expression will use similar but not identical aptitudes and skills. Cartooning, in many instances a form of social commentary, will use inductive reasoning, the aptitude of the critic. Imagination is evident in the work of many artists and is of help in teaching and writing.

ATOMIC RESEARCH

The subjective person is a specialist, working with a singleness of aim. The diagnostic-thinking specialist is often attracted to research of some kind but it is three-dimensional thinking that draws the research-minded person into research of a scientific nature.

The visualization in atomic research is about all that can be experienced, in contrast to architecture, where the end product brings into visible form the visualized structure.

Included in the various processes connected with nuclear energy are the mining, milling, and refining of uranium-bearing ores, the production of nuclear fuels, the manufacture of nuclear reactors, the design and construction of nuclear facilities, the operation of reactors, disposal of radioactive wastes, and processing of radioisotopes.

Physicists and chemists predominate, but mathematicians, biologists, and metallurgists engage in basic and applied research. Large numbers of technicians are involved in research, in testing materials, and as radiation monitors. Mechanics, machinists, electricians, pipefitters, and other skilled workers are engaged in the fabrication and maintenance of the machinery and equipment.

BIOLOGY

All of the sciences tend to attract subjective people with structural visualization. In each science, research tends to draw those with reasoning ability. Management positions, where any degree of forcefulness is needed, appeal to the objective person. Do you think a biologist would benefit from having a good memory for designs and forms?

Human variables other than aptitudes may influence the choice of an occupation. In a survey of 475 college students studying the sciences, the common interest of all the major groups in "Discovering new facts, solving problems, doing research, and making controlled observations" did not extend to the area of outdoor activities, described as "Being outdoors mostly, dealing with plants and animals." Only the biological science majors rated high in this area.

The biologist studies the origin, development, anatomy, function, distribution and other basic principles of plants and animals. Specializations abound in biology as in all of the other natural and physical sciences.

Biological science may be coupled with other scientific fields to explore problems requiring an interdisciplinary approach as in biochemistry and biophysics. Space exploration has brought the latest addition to the field of biology, exobiology, the study of evidence that some form of life exists elsewhere in the universe. Carl Sagan, director of planetary studies at Cornell University, states that "The idea of extraterrestrial life is an idea whose time has come."

CHEMISTRY

Chemists usually concentrate their work in one of the five main branches of chemistry: organic, inorganic, physical, analytical, or biochemistry. Chemistry is a servant science, having an impact on every field. New materials are available for architecture and engineering as a result of research.

Ecology and pollution are of growing concern. Where the origins have been chemical, the solution will be chemical also. Chemists will replace dangerous pesticides with ones that can do their job and degenerate to harmless materials. Chemists are eliminating air pollutants by revamping solvents, fuels, and disposal of trash. Chemists can demonstrate the commercial feasibility of the concept of total recycling of materials, leaving only yesterday's ideas to be thrown away.

You can see that there is a great variation in the nature of jobs within each occupation and that you don't need a rigid pattern of aptitudes. Do you think that finger dexterity would be of help in some of the work done by chemists? What other aptitudes would find an outlet in chemistry?

CLERGY

Although the language of aptitudes contains no words to explain the calling of the religious life, it is known that a wide diversity exists among those who enter it. Anything that you have can find an outlet here, a fitting situation that agrees with the belief that all of us are equal in the eyes of the Almighty.

Variations in aptitudes fill the needs of various congregations. New, expanding groups call for organizers and fund raisers, followed by builders. Other, more established groups need the teacher, philosopher, or theologian. Ailing groups require the services of a diagnostician.

Preparation for the clergy varies greatly from no formal educational requirements for some religious groups, to three or more years of study following college graduation. As a consequence, vocabulary levels range from low to high, permitting the matching of an individual with a compatible group.

Related occupations offer additional career opportunities in religious work: missionary, teacher, educational director, youth director, editor of religious publications, music director, and recreation leader.

More than with any other occupation, the work of a clergyman involves a total commitment to a way of life, yielding, with a few widely known exceptions, fewer financial rewards but bringing with it a profound sense of fulfillment.

DENTISTRY

Unless you are one of the rare people with perfect teeth, you have personal knowledge of what a dentist does. What aptitudes do you think would be helpful?

All dental schools approved by the American Dental Association require applicants to take the Dental Aptitude Test, which includes comprehension of scientific information, vocabulary and mathematics knowledge, visualization of three-dimensional patterns, and the use of hands and fingers in carving pieces of chalk to specified dimensions.

Dentistry has its general practitioners and specialists. Specialists devote their time to specific dental problems. Oral pathologists treat diseases of the mouth. Oral surgeons perform operations in the mouth and jaw. Orthodontists correct irregularities in the development of teeth and jaws by the use of braces and other devices. Endodontists perform root-canal therapy. Pedodontists specialize in the dental problems of children. Periodontists treat diseased tissues that support the teeth, and prosthodontists specialize in making artificial teeth and dentures. Support personnel include dental assistants, hygienists, and laboratory technicians.

ECONOMICS

Economics is the study of man's behavior in producing, exchanging, and consuming material goods and services. Economists in government carry out studies for use in assessing the need for changes in policy, regulations, and taxes. Economists employed by business firms provide management with information for making decisions on the advisability of adding new lines of merchandise, opening new branch operations, or otherwise expanding the company's business. More than half of the country's economists are employed by industry and business. Economics is a thinking occupation. The statistical work involved usually is done by computer operators.

The agricultural economists investigate the production and marketing of farm products in order to increase the efficiency of farm management, improve farm income, and effect favorable legislation. They forecast production and recommend improvements in financing.

The financial economist develops monetary policies and forecasts financial activity and examines credit structures, banking procedures, and interest rates. The international economist is concerned with tariffs, trade controls, cartels, and foreign investments. The labor economist attempts to forecast labor trends and recommends policies on the subjects of legislation, insurance, industrial accidents, and labor unions.

The study of consumer economics can be applied in a practical way to the problems of finding credit, setting up a budget, planning an insurance program, and financial investments.

GEOGRAPHY

Geographers study the spatial characteristics of the earth's terrain, minerals, soils, water, vegetation, and climate, relating them to where people live, why they are located there, and how they earn a living.

Research in physical geography includes the analysis of landforms, climate, soils, and natural resources. An economic geographer studies the distribution of agriculture, manufacturing, trade, transportation, and marketing systems. Political geography is the study of the way in which political processes are related to geographic boundaries and conditions. Cartographers make maps and compile the necessary data for them. Photogrammetry, the surveying of large areas by means of photographs, has enlarged its scope with the advent of space satellites equipped with cameras

Among the major agencies of the Federal government employing specialists in geography are the United States Army Topographic Command, the Department of the Interior, and the Department of Commerce. State and local governments also employ geographers, mostly on planning and development concessions. Geographers in private industry work for marketing research organizations, map companies, textbook publishers, travel agencies, manufacturing firms, and research institutes. A few work as map librarians. Geography includes a lot of territory, doesn't it?

MATHEMATICS

You have had enough exposure to mathematics over a period of years to give you some idea of what mathematicians do. Most of the people working in this occupation use their knowledge as a tool in the solution of practical problems in the sciences, in business, and in industry. They work on problems ranging from the stability of rockets to the effects of new drugs on disease.

Training in the field where mathematics will be applied is important. Fields of application include physics, engineering, management, economics, statistics, chemistry, astronomy, and biology, as well as computers. You can see that low structural visualization would be suited to some of the applications while structural thinking would be helpful in others.

Three universities offer an unusual curriculum in applied mathematics. Geodesy is the branch of applied mathematics that determines the shape of the earth. Geodetic studies can locate exact points on the surface of the earth.

Theoretical mathematicians deal with pure and abstract mathematical concepts without concern for the practical application of their work to everyday problems. They work toward the advancement of mathematical knowledge, the logical development of mathematical systems, and the analysis of relationships among mathematical forms.

PRINTING

One of our chief means of communication, printing is an art and a leading industry. More than 60 kinds of work are performed in the printing industry by people with all kinds of aptitudes.

You can study graphic communications, a high-vocabulary term for printing, in a four-year college curriculum and enter the printing field at an upper level, or you can enter with less education and work up as you gain experience.

The aptitudes used in printing depend on what special type of work you will be doing but, in the opinion of one veteran printer, any of the following would be of help: color perception, structural visualization, memory for design, art judgment, finger dexterity, tweezer dexterity, analytical reasoning, inductive reasoning, and number memory. The printer hastens to add that a good knowledge of spelling, punctuation, and grammar are essential in this occupation, which is literary as well as artistic, scientific, and mechanical.

ZOOLOGY

Zoology is the animal division of biology, with divisions of its own. Listed below are some of the areas of concentration.

Bacteriology	bacteria
Embryology	formation and development of embryos
Entomology	insects
Hematology	blood and its diseases

Herpetology	reptiles and amphibians
Histology	microscopic study of tissue structure
Ichthyology	fishes
Invertebrates	animals with no spinal column
Mammalogy	animals fed with milk of mothers
Morphology	form and structure of animals
Ornithology	birds
Parasitology	animals living in or on other animals
Pathology	diseased tissue
Vertebrates	animals with spinal columns

It is hoped that the short sketches presented above may suggest to you an approach to take in analyzing other fields of work. As a further aid, we have included below descriptions of more than forty different careers.

ACCOUNTANT

Job Description

Accountants prepare financial statements, give financial advice, and compile, analyze, examine, and verify financial reports, such as profit-and-loss statements, balance sheets, and tax reports.

Accountants work for the public, companies, and government. Public accountants work for, or own, independent accounting firms. They prepare financial statements for individuals or businesses. Management accountants handle financial statements for the companies they work for. Government accountants verify and maintain the records of government agencies and audit individuals and private businesses whose financial dealings are subject to government regulations. Internal auditors check the accuracy of their businesses' financial statements and look for signs of waste, mismanagement, and fraud.

Accountants usually specialize in one aspect of accounting. Some concentrate on tax matters, for example, while others act as management consultants. Accountants may also give advice on how to manage assets more lucratively.

Educational Requirements

A minimum of a bachelor's degree in accounting or a closely related field. Many organizations prefer a master's degree in accounting or business administration with a concentration in accounting. The federal government requires four years of college or an equivalent combination of education and experience.

In most states, a certified public accountant (CPA) is the only accountant that is licensed and regulated. In order to receive a CPA certificate, the accountant must pass the Uniform CPA Examination given by each state and meet requirements of education and experience, including four years of college education.

College Subjects

Accounting procedures; accounting theory; business; computers; economics; mathematics; money and banking.

Aptitudes

If you scored high in number facility and graphoria, but not high in structural visualization, a career in accounting should be considered. Clearly, number facility, which measures your ability to perform arithmetic operations both quickly and accurately, would be an asset for an accountant. Graphoria, a test in visual perception that measures your speed and accuracy with paper and pencil tasks, is also an asset. Statistically, accountants have scored high in graphoria (which was once called the accounting aptitude). In one study, 80 percent of examinees who scored high in graphoria stayed in that profession for eight years or longer, while only 3 percent of those who scored low stayed for that length of time.

Although one lacking a high score in structural visualization (also known as the spatial aptitude) appears better suited to the profession of accounting than one who scores high, anyone possessing structural visualization who is interested in a career in accounting should consider the area of cost accounting. Working from a blueprint, the cost accountant predicts the cost of constructing a bridge, a dam, or a tunnel, or the cost of manufacturing a piece of electrical equipment, an automobile, or an airplane. The ability to see in one's mind not only the finished solid structure but the tools necessary for the process requires high structural visualization.

Although a low score in ideaphoria is helpful in many areas of accountancy, a high score in this aptitude should not in itself deter you from a career as an accountant; rather, you should consider such aspects of accountancy as the teaching of that subject, personnel recruitment, or consulting, which would provide an outlet for your ideaphoria.

Personality should also be taken into consideration when determining the area of accounting that would best suit you. If you scored subjective in personality on the word-association test, you probably prefer working as an individual, relying on your skills and knowledge, rather than in working with groups or as part of a group. Being a consultant, having people come to you for advice, would be an example of what we mean. But if you scored objective in personality, you should function well in a position that requires group contact. A position as a manager in the accounting department of a firm, or that of financial officer, would use your numerical aptitudes, accounting experience, and personality.

ACTUARY

Job Description

Actuaries apply their knowledge of mathematics, statistics, and probability, as well as principles of finance and business, to problems in life, health, and casualty insurance, annuities, and premiums. They determine mortality, accident, sickness, disability, and retirement rates. In addition, they construct probability tables regarding such things as fires, natural disasters, and unemployment. These tables are based on the actuary's analysis of statistical data and other pertinent information.

Actuaries also design and review pension and insurance plans and calculate premiums. They may also calculate a company's assets and liabilities to ensure the payment of future benefits. When there are surplus earnings from insurance and annuity contracts, actuaries may determine methods that will ensure the equitable distribution of the funds.

Over sixty percent of all actuaries work for companies that sell life insurance. Others specialize in such areas as health, pension, or property insurance. Actuaries must be constantly aware of developments in business, legislation, health, and other areas that may affect insurance policies.

Educational Requirements

A four-year bachelor of science degree in mathematics or statistics, or a degree in business or economics with a heavy emphasis on mathematics or statistics. Very few colleges offer degrees in actuarial science.

To obtain full professional status, actuaries must successfully complete ten examinations administered by one of the professional societies of actuaries. The examinations cover mathematics and all aspects of the insurance business. The first examinations may be taken in college; the final tests are taken during employment in junior actuarial positions. Completion of all ten examinations, which require extensive home study, may take as long as five to ten years.

College Subjects

Accounting; algebra; analytical geometry; calculus; computer science; economics; insurance; statistics; science; probability; trigonometry.

Aptitudes

You should consider becoming an actuary—a career that demands a strong background in mathematics—if you scored high in graphoria, number series, analytical reasoning, and structural visualization. Speed and accuracy with paper and pencil tasks (high graphoria), as measured by the number-checking test, is an important aptitude for actuaries, because they work almost exclusively with numbers. In addition, the ability to use numerical information to solve problems, as measured by the number-series test, is an important aptitude for actuaries and other individuals who analyze quantitative information to make decisions or recommendations. Actuaries analyze numerical information in order to compile premium rates, and they analyze statistics to calculate, for example, probabilities of death, unemployment, retirement, and property loss.

Considering the complexity of actuarial work, it is also important for an individual seeking a career in this field to be able to organize information in a logical way or sequence. Thus, a high score on the analytical-reasoning test would be a major asset. This is even more true today than in the past, because of the widespread use of computers in the actuarial field and the need for some actuaries to be involved in the programming of actuarial software and in systems analysis.

Statistically, actuaries have also scored high in structural visualization. This aptitude has long been a predictor of performance on the mathematics portion of the Scholastic Aptitude Test.

There are many different aspects to actuarial work, so individuals who score either subjective or objective in personality on the word-association test can function well in this field. If you scored subjective—an indication that you might prefer working as an individual—you might do well in such introductory positions as preparing tabulations for actuarial tables. Later in your career, your subjective personality could enable you to work as a consultant, with people coming to you for advice. On the other hand, if you scored objective—an indication that you prefer working with or through other individuals—you might strive for a position in which you supervise actuarial clerks, or in which you work with a research team.

If you scored high in ideaphoria, the teaching of actuarial science would provide an outlet for that aptitude, as would positions in which your responsibilities included such activities as the development of plans for new lines of business and the writing about legislation that affects the insurance industry.

ADMINISTRATIVE SERVICES MANAGER

Job Description

Administrative services managers oversee and direct staffs that are involved in support services in both business and government. There are many different kinds of administrative services, and they include: secretarial and correspondence work; the processing of financial and personnel records; information processing; communication; conference planning and travel; mail; materials scheduling and distribution; printing; data processing; library; food; and transportation.

The managers of these services develop overall plans, set goals and deadlines, and develop procedures to improve these services.

An administrative services manager in a small organization usually oversees all supportive services. In larger firms, however, there are generally two or more administrative service managers who specialize in one or more of these support services.

Educational Requirements

The educational requirements of an administrative services manager vary from company to company and are also determined by the educational needs of the specific administrative service.

Most administrative services managers work for several years in various administrative services before becoming managers. In some areas—secretarial, mail room, and similar administrative support activities, for example—employers may require only a high school diploma. Most employers, however, prefer a two-year associate of arts degree in business or management. For those who manage such technical activities as audiovisual and graphics services, employers usually prefer that the individual have post-secondary technical school training. And for managers of such highly complex services as contract administration, employers require a bachelor's degree, preferably in business administration. A bachelor's degree generally improves an administrative manager's chances of advancing to a mid-level management position and then to a top-level management position.

Some administrative services managers with the proper experience establish their own management consulting or management services firm.

College Subjects

Office technology; accounting; business mathematics; computer applications; business law. In addition, administrative services managers should take courses in those areas in which they specialize. Those who manage a corporate library, for example, should take courses in, or obtain a degree in, library science.

Aptitudes

If you scored high in graphoria but not high in structural visualization, and if you are objective in personality, you might consider a career as an administrative services manager.

Graphoria, a measure of perceptual speed, is useful in doing the clerical aspects of the work. It also comes into play when the administrative services manager reviews reports and other written materials prepared by subordinates.

Administrative services managers must maintain regular communication and contact with their superiors, subordinates, individuals in other departments, and a host of professionals. They sometimes interview prospective employees, train them after they are hired, and plan, oversee, and evaluate their work. In addition, they must keep their supervisors informed of progress and problems. As a result, low structural visualization—an indication that the individual would prefer a career that entails the use of the oral and written word more than one that entails working with concrete things—is a major asset for administrative services managers, as is an objective personality—an indication that the individual is able to function well working with a group.

ADVERTISING ACCOUNT EXECUTIVE

Job Description

Account executives plan and direct advertising campaigns for clients of their advertising agency. They oversee the four main steps in the advertising process: research, such as determining who the customers will be and how the product compares with competitive products; the selection of the media—newspapers, magazines, radio, or television; the creation of the advertisement—a layout for a print advertisement, a script for a radio commercial, or a storyboard for a television commercial; and the production of the actual advertisement that will be read or seen by consumers.

During these steps, account executives may supervise the activities of artists, copywriters, market researchers, media planners, photographers, musicians, moviemakers, actors, and many other media-production specialists.

Account executives first confer with clients to determine their advertising requirements, such as their media preferences and budgetary limitations. They then develop an advertising plan or campaign, which must be approved by the client. They carry out the campaign by coordinating activities of workers who engage in artwork

75

layout, copywriting, developing special displays, purchasing media time, and space and market research. They attend regular meetings with clients to report progress, and they go on location to oversee the production of television or radio advertisement.

Account executives are employed by advertising agencies. They are responsible for seeing that the ad campaign is on time and on budget. As a result, they are constantly under pressure to meet deadlines, and their working hours are generally long and irregular.

Educational Requirements

A four-year bachelor's degree in marketing, business administration, or liberal arts, coupled with work experience in advertising, sales, or marketing is required by most employers. Account executives usually begin as copywriters, market researchers, or media planners and advance to the position of account executive. Some advertising agencies offer employees account-managing training programs.

College Subjects

Managerial finance; marketing; product planning and promotion; interpersonal and organizational communication; economics; media; psychology; advertising; business administration.

Aptitudes

Advertising account executives plan and supervise advertising campaigns; they are the people at advertising agencies who get things done. In a real sense, they serve two organizations—their agency and their agency's client. This is because their goal is not only to ensure that their agency is making a profit, but that all of the agency's resources are being used in the best possible way for the benefit of the client.

You might consider a career in this field if you scored high in ideaphoria but not high in structural visualization, and if you scored objective in personality on the word-association test. This cluster of aptitudes is considered a group-influencing pattern, and it is an asset for individuals who are responsible for selling their product, the advertising campaign, to the agency's clients.

High ideaphoria, the ability to come up with a rapid flow of ideas, clearly is helpful for an individual in the creative areas of advertising. An account executive, some of whom start out as copy writers or artists, must often contribute ideas to the agency's creative people, as well as evaluate their ideas.

Low structural visualization goes hand in hand with high ideaphoria in this career field, because individuals who score low are more comfortable when they are dealing with intangibles than with concrete things.

Because the account executive is responsible for the success of the work of the agency's creative people, an objective score in personality on the word-association test, which indicates an ability to function well as a part of a group, is an asset.

ADVERTISING ART DIRECTOR

Job Description
Art directors develop concepts and oversee the design of layouts for advertisements that appear in books, magazines, and newspapers, on packaging and posters, and on television. Their aim is to create artwork that both illustrates and adorns subject matter that promotes the use of the products or services offered by the client.

Art directors first determine a design concept and then sketch rough plans for the advertisement. In doing so, they must take into account budget restraints and the client's preference with regard to presentation approach, technique, and style. Upon approval by the client or the advertising agency's account executive, art directors assign work to artists, photographers, layout artists, and other specialists. Art directors then review the layouts, make whatever changes are needed, and present the final layout to the account executive or client for approval .

Many art directors specialize in such areas as print media, the design of packaging and promotional displays for new products, or the design of company logos or stationery.

Educational Requirements
A bachelor or associate degree is generally required for positions as an art director or manager of an art design department in an

advertising agency. A portfolio, or a collection of the art director's best works, including handmade, computer-generated, or printed examples, is usually required to show the extent of the individual's experience and education.

The skills needed to learn the basics of design, and the skills needed to assemble an attractive portfolio, can be learned by completing a bachelor's degree in graphic arts or applied design.

College Subjects

Calligraphy; color harmony; printmaking; graphic arts; layout; life drawing; spatial organization; freehand and mechanical drawing; business administration; computer-aided design; designing and sketching; quality control; materials.

Aptitudes

You might pursue a career as an art director in the field of advertising if you scored high in ideaphoria but not high in structural visualization, and if you scored objective in personality on the word-association test. This cluster of aptitudes, which is considered a group-influencing pattern, is an asset for art directors because they must sell their designs and concepts to their agency's account executives. In addition, they are sometimes called upon to work with the account executives in selling the concept to the agency's clients.

Memory for design is also a valuable trait in this profession, because hundreds of designs and design elements are worked with on a daily basis.

An ability to function well as a leader of a group is another important trait for advertising art directors, because they are responsible for the success of the work of the artists, photographers, and other creative people who work for them. An objective score in personality on the world-association test is an indication of this ability.

ADVERTISING COPYWRITER

Job Description

Advertising copywriters write copy, or text, for advertisements that are published in such media as newspapers, magazines, and brochures, and for commercials that are broadcast on radio or television. The purpose of the copy is to promote the sale of goods and services.

Advertising copywriters are for the most part idea generators. They turn informational and promotional ideas into words that appear in articles, bulletins, advertisements, sales letters, and speeches. They select and organize the information and put it into words that they hope will cause the reader to react in a desired way.

Advertising copywriters first discuss the style and length of the advertisement with marketing representatives, sales personnel, and others. Through interviews and research, they obtain more information about the product. They also study consumer surveys and advertising trends before developing a formal presentation approach. Copywriters create preliminary drafts of the copy, including slogans, headlines, and text, and then submit them to the supervisor for approval. Copywriters revise the copy as many times as necessary. They work closely with advertising art directors and account executives.

Educational Requirements

A college degree in communications, marketing, or English is usually required. Employers prefer that applicants have prior experience with high school, college, and community newspapers, and radio and television stations. More important is the ability to develop original and exciting ideas. Familiarity with electronic publishing, graphics, and video production equipment is useful.

College Subjects

English; business administration; communications; sociology; psychology; computers; publishing; history; market research; statistics; advertising.

Aptitudes

Ideaphoria, the ability to produce a rapid flow of ideas, is the most important aptitude for an individual who wants to pursue a career as an advertising copywriter. The advertising copywriter must produce eye-catching headlines and interesting and informative copy for print advertising. He or she must write scripts and jingles for radio and television commercials. And not only must a copywriter produce copy that is fresh and exciting, but he or she must be able to produce it in great quantity, because most of it will be rejected by the agency's creative director or by the client before the final copy is approved.

The score in structural visualization should also be taken into consideration by an individual seeking a career as an advertising copywriter. A low score is indicative of an individual's ability to function better in the world of words than in the world of concrete things, so this trait goes hand in hand with ideaphoria.

There are opportunities in the field of advertising copywriting for those who score either objective or subjective in personality on the word-association test. One who scores objective—an indication of an ability to work compatibly with others—would function well working with the art director and other members of the advertising agency's creative team, or perhaps as the chief copywriter responsible for the creative output of junior copywriters. One who scores subjective, however, might prefer work that was more individual in nature. Freelance copywriting, the supplying of text on request to an advertising agency, but with minimal involvement in the meetings of the agency's creative group, is but one example of work of an individual nature that might be suited to an individual with a subjective personality.

ARCHAEOLOGIST

Job Description
Archaeologists study the characteristics and history of cultures of the past. By obtaining pottery, tools, figures, and other artistic and cultural artifacts during digs, explorations, or excavations, they derive information about such cultural and social developments of the society as social structure, customs, and food-gathering techniques.

Archaeologists gather artifacts and other buried remains by excavation. They study and interpret them in order to establish the approximate age and cultural identity. One of the archaeologist's main goals is to determine the chronological sequence and development of various cultures. They are especially interested in those peoples and events that led to more advanced levels of existence.

Depending on the excavation site being studied, archaeologists may travel to distant areas and work in uncomfortable, sometimes primitive surroundings. A significant amount of time may be spent doing field work, including overseeing efforts to excavate sites. But most of an archaeologist's work is in the laboratory, where the artifacts that are found are catalogued, measured, analyzed, and described.

Some archaeologists, known as classical archaeologists, concentrate on the major civilizations of the Near and Middle East. Those who study the past cultures of the Columbian history of the Americas may be designated historical archaeologists. Other areas of specialization include the Indians of the American Southwest and the classical Greeks and Romans. Still other archaeologists concentrate on broad areas of subject matter, such as colonial or medieval archaeology.

Educational Requirements

A master's degree is the minimum requirement for work as an archaeologist. Junior Colleges will accept applications for teaching jobs from people with master's degrees in the social sciences. A Ph.D. is the minimum requirement for most teaching positions in colleges and universities as well for positions in research and field work. Those with bachelor degrees can qualify as research assistants or administrative aides.

College Subjects

Cultural anthropology; earth science; chemistry; biology; ethnology; linguistics; mathematics; history; art history; anthropology; statistics; geography; computer science; sociology.

Aptitudes

If you score high in structural visualization, inductive reasoning, and memory for design, a career in archaeology will provide an outlet for these traits. An individual with high structural visualization—an engineer, for example—can picture in his mind the structure of three-dimensional forms; he can tell how something drawn as a blueprint will look when it is eventually built. An archaeologist also requires high structural visualization, but his mental process is almost the opposite of that of the engineer: He must be able to look at the excavated ruins of an ancient civilization and be able to draw an architect's plan of the houses and other structures.

Inductive reasoning—the ability to reason from the particular to the general and draw a conclusion—is the trait that enables archaeologists to study a variety of artifacts and develop a theory about how an ancient group of people lived and worked.

The ability to remember designs is also a valuable trait. Memory for design helps archaeologists to remember not only different styles of architecture but also the thousands of different elements that make up the design of homes or other buildings. The ability to remember the various elements and aspects of an archaeological site will also help the archaeologist when writing a report about his findings.

Archaeology also offers an outlet for ideaphoria, the ability to produce a rapid flow of ideas, when the archaeologist teaches the subject or when he or she speculates about particular finds.

The field of archaeology has opportunities for those who score either subjective or objective in personality on the word-association test. One who scores subjective might prefer work of an individual nature, such as cleaning, mending, and restoring artifacts. One who scores objective, however—an indication of an ability to work well with or through other individuals—might prefer working as part of a team at an excavation site. An objective person would also be able to function well when dealing with organizations or institutions that might sponsor his field work.

ARCHITECT

Job Description

Architects plan, design, and supervise the construction, alteration, and repair of buildings, such as private residences, office buildings, theaters, public buildings, and factories. Their aim is to make the buildings functional, safe, economical, and pleasing to the eye.

Architects first consult with their clients to determine functional and space requirements. They then prepare information about design, specifications, materials, equipment, and estimated costs and time. Preliminary plans are then drawn up; if the client approves, and a final design is agreed upon, that design is translated into scale and full-size working drawings which show the details of the proposed structure.

Architects also assist their clients in obtaining bids from building contractors and awarding construction contracts. They then supervise the administration of the construction contracts and conduct on-site observations of the work in progress.

Some architects concentrate on the design aspects of the project, others on the engineering aspects. Many architects specialize: some design residential buildings, for example; others, commercial buildings; and still others, shopping centers.

Educational Requirements

A five-year bachelor of architecture degree, with the first two years consisting of liberal arts courses. Many graduate architects then go on to take a two-year master's program. An alternate course of study is a four-year liberal arts degree followed by a three- or four-year master's program in architecture.

All states require that practicing architects be licensed. Architects who have graduated from an accredited school of architecture and who have had at least three years of practical experience in an architectural firm may take the four-day Architect Registration Examination, which is administered by state licensing boards.

College Subjects

Architectural design; architectural graphics; structural theory; specification writing; freehand drawing; history and theory of architecture; building design; urban planning.

Aptitudes

The most important aptitudes for architects are high structural visualization and memory for design. An individual with high structural visualization can picture in his mind the structure of three-dimensional forms; he can tell how something drawn as a blueprint will look when it is eventually built.

Today, computer-assisted design is increasingly used in the field of architecture.Some of the more sophisticated computer programs enable the architect to see his or her plans in three dimensions, but this is basically a system for making routine work easier, so high structural visualization is still a major asset. In addition, high structural visualization is useful in mathematics, and mathematical skills are necessary in architecture.

The ability to remember designs is also a valuable characteristic, because it helps helps architects to remember not only different styles of architecture but also the thousands of different elements that make up the design of homes, theaters, or other buildings. The ability to remember the various elements and aspects of an architectural site will also help the architect create a structure that will fit naturally into that site in a way that is harmonious with the environment.

The field of architecture has opportunities for those who score either subjective or objective in personality on the word-association test. One who scores subjective might prefer work of an individual nature, such as sitting at a drafting table or in front of a computer designing buildings or parts of buildings. One who scores objective, however—an indication of an ability to work compatibly with others—might prefer working as part of a design team or in the field, supervising contractors, plumbers, carpenters, painters, and others. An objective person would also be able to function well in situations that involve dealing directly with the client, for the architect must be able to interact with the client in such a way that he or she can translate the client's needs into reality.

ARCHIVIST

Job Description

Archivists maintain and safeguard permanent and public records and historically valuable documents. During the course of their work, they search for, acquire, analyze, appraise, edit, and describe these records and documents. They often make the documents available for reference. Some archivists also oversee the restoration of documents.

Archivists analyze vast amounts of information, such as government records, correspondence from famous persons, and minutes of corporate board meetings. They determine what should be made part of a historical record or put on exhibit. They catalog records, alphabetically and chronologically, and decide whether they should be stored on computers or microfilm or kept as original documents. They may also determine the value of documents by researching, for example, the date of the writing and the names of the author and original recipient.

Many archivists work for, or act as advisers to, government agencies, educational institutions, corporations, and other organizations that conduct research. They supply the documentation as well as such relevant information as the economic, political, military, and social history of the time period in which the documents were written. Archivists may also take part in educational and public-service activities, such as teaching, lecturing, and supervising workshops.

Some archivists specialize in one specific area of history or technology. Others specialize in a specific type of record, such as manuscripts, photographs, sound recordings, or motion pictures.

Educational Requirements

A four-year bachelor of arts degree in history with courses in archival or library science. Many archivists also obtain a master's degree or a doctorate. Employment as an archivist usually requires graduate training and several years of on-the-job work experience.

College Subjects

English; archival science; history; political science; mathematics; library science; business; accounting; bookkeeping.

Aptitudes

Because the acquisition, description, and cataloging of records, documents, and other items of lasting value constitute an important part of an archivist's work, graphoria is an important aptitude for any one interested in pursuing a career in this field. A high score in graphoria—as measured by the number-checking test—indicates that the individual would be able to work speedily and accurately with these paper and pencil tasks.

The variety of subject matter dealt with by archivists is vast, so a large vocabulary would be useful in this field. In addition, a large vocabulary is not only essential for gaining knowledge in this field, but also for making the full use of your other aptitudes possible. Low structural visualization, an indication that the individual would enjoy working in a field in which words, rather than concrete things, are important, would complement a large vocabulary.

Scoring subjective in personality on the word-association test would also be helpful to those interested in the archival field, because this indicates a preference for working as an individual rather than as a member of a group. An archivist must constantly accumulate knowledge about his or her particular area of specialty, and this is most often done as an individual, rather than as a member of a group.

ART HISTORIAN

Job Description

Art historians research, study, and analyze artists and the works of artists of the past and the present. They prepare chronological accounts, records, or outlines of artwork by individual artists or of artwork produced by social, ethnic, geographic, and other groups.

Art historians examine all aspects of artwork created in the past, including how the artists lived and the ideologies of the time period. They assemble historical data through research in archives, historical indexes and catalogs, texts and documents, diaries, news files, and other published and unpublished materials. They organize and evaluate the data based on its authenticity, relativity, and significance.

Art historians may conduct research for individuals, institutions, or commercial organizations. They compile data on artists and artworks, as well as on the manners and customs of specific historical periods. They may also oversee the study, preservation, restoration, and exhibition of artworks and artifacts.

Most art historians teach and do research in colleges and universities. Others work in archives, historical societies, libraries, museums, research organizations, and large corporations. Art historians usually specialize in a specific country, time period, or type of artwork, such as painting, sculpture, architecture, graphics, or the decorative arts.

Educational Requirements

A seven- or eight-year Ph.D. in art history is required for most positions in colleges, universities, research, or administration.

College Subjects

Art history; museum studies; arts administration; mathematics; painting; materials; fabrics.

Aptitudes

Memory for design is an especially helpful aptitude for those individuals interested in a career as an art historian. High memory for design clearly is an asset because art historians deal primarily with visual materials, such as graphics, paintings, architectural plans, photographs, and architecture. The ability to recall the details of a particular piece of prehistoric artwork, for example, is helpful in placing that work in its proper chronological time frame and in its correct geographical location.

Some art historians may at times work directly with three-dimensional objects—they may oversee, for example, an exhibition of architectural artifacts. But for the most part, their occupation deals more with words than with concrete things, so a low score in structural visualization would be more of an asset than a high one.

An art historian must constantly accumulate knowledge about his or her particular area of specialty. Much of this work is done individually, rather than as a member of a group. As a result, a subjective score in personality on the word-association test—an indication that you might prefer working as an individual rather than as a member of a group—would also be an asset.

BANK OFFICER

Job Description

Bank officers plan, develop, and direct the public relations and financial policies and practices of banks, mortgage banking companies, personal credit institutions, savings and loan associations, and trust companies. Their aim is to ensure that institutional objectives, goals, and financial expectations are met and that they are in compliance with government regulations and board recommendations.

Bank officers coordinate communication between branch offices, departments, and divisions to ensure that vital information needed for efficient daily operations is available. They also delegate authority and responsibility to subordinate officers, who concentrate on such customer services as the transfer of money between accounts and the planning and implementation of various bank activities and operations. The bank officer ultimately reviews financial statements and reports to determine policy changes resulting from customer demand or changes in economic conditions.

Some bank officers concentrate on financial document preparation, others on customer service or public relations. Many bankers specialize: some become mortgage or trust management bankers; others, correspondence bankers.

Still other bank officers become loan officers. Loan officers service individuals and businesses that are seeking to borrow money from banks for the purchase of such personal items as cars, boats, and homes, and for the purchase of commercial real estate and for other business purposes. The loan officers evaluate, examine, recommend and authorize credit. They also advise borrowers on their financial status and methods of payment.

Loan officers first review the loan application for completeness. They then analyze the applicant's financial status to determine his ability to repay the loan. Loan officers can either approve the loan or refer the loan application to a loan committee for approval. Once the loan is accepted, the loan officer completes the loan agreement and arranges repayment schedules. Loan officers may also buy and sell loans, contracts, or foreclosed real estate.

In larger banks, installment loan officers handle personal loans, and commercial loan officers handle business loans. In smaller banks, general loan officers usually handle both types of loans.

Educational Requirements

A four-year bachelor's degree in accounting, business, finance, or economics is usually required for consideration as a management trainee. Because of the increasing internationalization of business, a second language such as German or Japanese is helpful. Some banks promote from within and train tellers and clerks for positions as officers. Most larger banks have middle-management training programs lasting at least six months.

College Subjects

Accounting and budget management; economics; financial analysis; business administration; data processing; corporate cash management; international banking; managerial finance; economics; money and banking; organizational behavior; statistics.

Aptitudes

If you scored high in number facility and graphoria, but not high in structural visualization, you might consider a career in banking. Number facility, the ability to perform arithmetic operations both quickly and accurately, is certainly an asset for a bank officer, as is graphoria—speed and accuracy with paper and pencil tasks.

A score in structural visualization that is not high is an asset because this indicates that the individual is more comfortable dealing with intangibles than with concrete things. In addition, those bank officers who score high in ideaphoria would use this aptitude when engaging in public relations activities for the bank.

CONSTRUCTION MANAGER

Job Description

Construction managers, who are also known as construction superintendents, production managers, or general contractors, are responsible for the construction of all types of structures, from small one-family homes to large industrial complexes.

Construction managers may be self-employed or they may work as salaried employees for construction companies. Those who oversee the building of small homes or other structures are usually self-employed, and they directly oversee the work of the various construction workers employed for the project. Construction managers who work on large projects, such as the construction of skyscrapers, industrial complexes, or shopping malls, usually work for large construction companies.

Managers of large projects have overall responsibility, but do not engage in the day-to-day supervision of the construction trade workers. Rather, that responsibility is delegated to lower-level construction supervisors or managers who oversee the various stages involved in creating a structure. These stages include, for example, site preparation, the installation of sewage systems, landscaping, road construction, the construction of the building's framework, and the installation of floors, walls, and roofs. Other construction managers might oversee the necessary carpentry, electrical work, and plumbing, as well as the installation of air-conditioning and heating systems.

In addition, construction managers help determine which

construction methods will be used and what labor is required. They also schedule the work, monitor the progress of the construction, and ensure that all necessary licenses and permits are obtained.

Educational Requirements

Many individuals have started out in the construction trades as craft workers—as plumbers, electricians, carpenters, or masons, for example—and, after displaying supervisory capability, advanced to the position of construction manager for a small or medium-sized contractor. Similarly, individuals who have obtained degrees in engineering, architecture, cost estimating, or other related fields have become construction managers.

Today, however, many construction firms prefer that their construction managers have a bachelor's degree in construction management. A master's degree in construction management improves one's chances of obtaining a senior position with a large construction firm.

College Subjects

Project control and development; site planning; building design; building codes and standards; construction materials; construction methods; scheduling; cost estimating; contract administration; inspection procedures; engineering; architecture; mathematics; statistics; computer science.

Aptitudes

Structural visualization, the ability to picture in one's mind the structure of three-dimensional forms, is the single-most important aptitude for an individual seeking a career as a construction manager. This aptitude enables the individual to look at blueprints and building plans and visualize what the finished structure will look like and how the various elements of the structure fit together.

Because much of a construction manager's work involves budgeting and scheduling and requires great attention to detail, an average or high score in graphoria—a measure of one's speed and accuracy with paper and pencil tasks—would certainly be an advantage. If the individual lacks graphoria, he could still work as a construction manager, but he would be well advised to delegate much of the budgeting and scheduling work to someone who scores average or high in this trait.

One who scores objective in personality on the word-association test would find an outlet for this characteristic as a construction manager, because the work involves almost constant contact with many other individuals, from construction workers and cost estimators, to engineers, architects, and project owners.

CONSTRUCTION TRADES WORKERS

Job Description
The talents and skills of many people are needed to construct a building or any other kind of structure. Architects and engineers design them, and contractors or construction managers bring together the materials and people that are necessary to do the job. But the physical work of erecting the building and finishing it to the specifications of the owner is done by a variety of construction trades craft workers

Construction trades workers do everything from excavating the site of the building, pouring the foundation, and erecting the framework to installing the interior walls, electrical wiring, cabinets, and carpeting. There are many individuals who can do more than one of these tasks, but for the most part, construction trades workers specialize in one particular trade.

All of the construction trades professions, to one degree or another, require manual dexterity, stamina, and strength.

Many construction trades workers are self-employed, but most work for building contractors. The type of work entailed in some of their trades is detailed below.

Bricklayers and *stonemasons* build and repair walls, floors, fireplaces, partitions, patios, walkways, and other structures using brick, cinder block, concrete block, stone, and a variety of other masonry materials.

Carpenters build and repair wooden structures. Those who practice "rough" carpentry erect the wooden frameworks of buildings, while those who practice "finish" carpentry install such items as cabinets, paneling, and moldings. Skilled carpenters can do both "rough" and "finish" carpentry.

Concrete masons use concrete—a mixture of cement, sand, gravel, and water—to build patios, driveways, and sidewalks.

Drywall workers create internal walls and ceilings in homes and other buildings by installing and finishing drywall panels to the wooden frameworks.

Electricians install electrical systems in homes and buildings. Such systems include those necessary for operating lighting, power, refrigeration, air-conditioning, and heating.

Floor-covering installers install carpeting, linoleum, tile, and other floor coverings.

Glaziers cut and install windows, mirrors, doors, display cases, and other products that are made out of glass, plastic, and other glass substitutes.

Insulation workers install insulating material in or around walls, ducts, pipes, boilers, and tanks in homes and buildings to prevent energy loss.

Painters apply paint, stain, varnish, lacquer, and other finishes to the surfaces of buildings in order to protect them and to make them more attractive.

Plumbers install, maintain, and repair various types of pipe systems, including those that carry water, gas, steam, and waste. They also install such plumbing fixtures as sinks, bathtubs, and toilets.

Roofers install and repair roofs covered with tile, slate, shingles, felt, tar, or other roofing materials.

Other construction trades workers include elevator constructors, lathers, paperhangers, plasterers, pipe fitters, sheet-metal workers, and ironworkers.

Educational Requirements

Most construction trades workers learn their craft informally through on-the-job training and through 2- to 4-year apprenticeship programs that are offered by employees and labor unions. While not necessary, a high school diploma or the equivalent is of some importance.

School Subjects

Vocational and shop courses; blueprint reading; applied mathematics; sketching; drafting; mechanical drawing; safety.

Aptitudes

High structural visualization—the ability to picture in one's mind the structure of three-dimensional forms—is a decided advantage for anyone seeking a career as a construction trades worker. Almost all such workers use blueprints or building plans at various times during their work, and the ability to comprehend the relationship between the plan and the finished structure is a major asset.

COST ESTIMATOR

Job Description

Cost estimators predict the cost of manufacturing and construction and the cost of goods and services. They gather information in order to help management competitively bid for contracts and to determine the price of various projects and services.

Cost estimators in the construction business first analyze a proposal to determine whether a bid should be made on the project. If interested, they visit the site or the production facility to determine material lists, production requirements, equipment purchases, crew sizes, and the availability of such services as electricity and water. They then formulate a final bid that includes allowances for shipping delays, overhead, taxes, and insurance. They submit the bid to the developer, who then decides which company to hire. After the bid is accepted, the cost estimator monitors the project.

Cost estimators who work for companies that take on large projects may specialize. Some concentrate on tool, fixture, and machinery costs, while others specialize in construction or manufacturing costs.

Educational Requirements

In construction work, which employs about two-thirds of all cost estimators, employers seek applicants who have work experience in materials, electrical work, and other specialties, as well as some post-secondary courses in engineering, operations research, statistics, or accounting. For beginning positions in the government, applicants must have a bachelor's degree with a major in engineering, business administration, economics, or a related subject.

Beginning cost estimators are usually involved in on-the-job-training. Certification is given to individuals who have worked at least three years and have passed written and oral examinations.

College Subjects

Managerial accounting; statistics; operations research; architectural engineering; applied economics; construction materials engineering; urban planning; labor practices; computer science; business administration; building design.

Aptitudes

If you scored high in number facility, graphoria, and structural visualization, you might consider a career as a cost estimator. Number facility, which measures your ability to perform arithmetic operations both quickly and accurately, is obviously an asset for a cost estimator. Graphoria—speed and accuracy with paper and pencil tasks—is also a valuable trait to possess.

High structural visualization is also important for cost estimators. Working from a blueprint, the cost estimator predicts the cost of constructing a bridge, a dam, or a tunnel, or the cost of manufacturing a piece of electrical equipment, a computer, an automobile, or an airplane. The ability to see in one's mind not only the finished solid structure but the tools necessary for the process requires high structural visualization.

COUNSELOR

Job Description

Counselors provide individual and group guidance services to people with educational, career, personal, and social problems. They collect, interpret, and apply scientific data to problems in human behavior and mental processes.

Counselors first collect information about individuals through counseling sessions, interviews, records, medical histories, tests, and professional sources. They organize and analyze the data and use it to determine the clients' abilities, aptitudes, interests, and personality characteristics.

Counselors then suggest remedial or corrective actions. They assist the individuals in making better adjustments and in implementing effective decision-making processes to help them overcome their social and emotional problems and achieve their vocational and educational objectives. They may also conduct research and follow-up activities to evaluate the effectiveness of the current counseling techniques and to develop new ones.

Some counselors concentrate on vocational problems, others on educational problems. Some become school counselors; others, rehabilitation counselors; and still others, counseling psychologists.

Educational Requirements

A two-year master's degree, including a period of supervised work experience in counseling, is required. Individuals with four-year bachelor degrees in such fields as career counseling or mental health counseling may qualify for employment, especially if they have experience in job placement, personnel, or social work. These individuals may not be eligible for certification or licensure, which is required by most states for counselors in private practice.

To be awarded the title "National Certified Counselor" by the National Board for Certified Counselors, an individual must have earned a master's degree in counseling, have at least two years of professional counseling experience, and pass the National Counselor Examination.

College Subjects

Individual and group counseling; psychology; communication; counseling theory and techniques; assessment and evaluation; career development; community resources.

Aptitudes

If you scored high in ideaphoria, you might consider a career as a counselor. Counseling is a people-oriented profession that requires constant communication between the counselor and the client. This career, as a result, offers an excellent outlet for ideaphoria, because the counselor who is able to produce a rapid flow of ideas will be better able to help people evaluate their interests and abilities. He or she will also be more effective in helping clients with their problems, whether they are personal, social, educational, or occupational. Low structural visualization, an indication that the individual is more comfortable in the world of words than in the world of concrete things, would complement ideaphoria.

The job of helping people with problems often uses inductive reasoning, the ability to reason from the particular to the general and to form a conclusion. Like physicians, counselors must be able to take a set of facts or observations and develop a theory that explains them. Mental health and rehabilitation counselors, especially, must be able to determine their clients' underlying problems.

DESIGNER, THREE-DIMENSIONAL

Job Description

The goal of designers of three-dimensional articles, products, and materials is to create useful and functional things. But, like fine artists, they also strive to make their creations beautiful. There are many interesting opportunities in this rewarding professional field for individuals with artistic talent.

Fashion or *clothing designers* design coats, suits, dresses, blouses, and other articles of clothing, as well as accessories such as gloves, shoes, handbags, and hats. Most fashion designers work for clothing manufacturing firms, where they may specialize in the design of men's, women's, or children's apparel.

Many fashion designers specialize even further, with some concentrating, for example, on swimwear, shoes, dresses, or suits. Related to fashion design is costume design, the creation of wardrobes for films, theater productions, television shows, operas, and ballets.

Furniture designers design chairs, tables, beds, desks, dressers, and other articles of furniture for use in homes, offices, schools, and elsewhere.

Industrial designers develop and design a wide range of machine-made products, such as computers, cars, home appliances, toys, writing utensils, scientific instruments, and farm, manufacturing, and transportation equipment.

Interior designers, often working closely with architects, plan, design, and furnish the interiors of residential and industrial buildings, as well as such commercial establishments as offices, hotels, and restaurants. They also prepare working drawings and specifications for interior construction, renovations, and additions. Especially for this aspect of the work, the interior designer must be knowledgeable about the basics of space planning, the structure of buildings, and the mechanical equipment used in buildings.

Those interior designers who specialize in the decorative aspects of the work—the selection and arrangement of furniture, floor coverings, draperies, artwork, and other adornments—are called interior decorators. Some designers specialize in the interior design of ships, planes, and automobiles.

Stage or set designers plan, develop, and prepare the sets for movies, television, and theater. They design and arrange objects and materials within sets so that they are aesthetically pleasing and functional and so that they transform the entire stage for each of the scenes in the production.

Other designers of three-dimensional articles, products, or materials include exhibition designers, who create displays for museums, art galleries, and exhibitions; floral designers, who arrange flowers and foliage into designs; and package designers, who create containers for cosmetics, cereals and other kinds of foods, and a multitude of other products.

Educational Requirements

Fashion designers should take a two- or three-year associate program at an art school or institute, or obtain a four-year bachelor of fine arts degree. Some fashion designers then go on to take a two-year's master's program. A good portfolio—a collection of the designer's best designs—is required for an entry-level job, as is knowledge about trends in the fashion world. On-the-job training for one to three years is recommended for beginners and is usually needed for advancement to higher positions.

Furniture designers should take a two-year program at an art institute or school. A four-year bachelor's degree in design is preferred for high-level advancement. Another way to learn furniture design is to complete a four-year apprenticeship, which includes on-the-job training and classroom instruction. A high school education or its equivalent is usually required for an apprenticeship.

Industrial designers are required to have a four- or five-year bachelor of science degree in industrial design, which is offered by art schools and by design or art departments at colleges and universities. Those with degrees in architecture, engineering, and fine arts may qualify as industrial designers if they have the appropriate talent and work experience. Experience with computer-aided design is especially important in this field.

Interior designers should take, as a minimum, a three-year program in a school of interior design. However, a four-year bachelor of arts program in fine arts with a major in interior design, combined with several years of design-related work experience, is needed to obtain membership in the American Institute of Interior Design or the National Society of Interior Design.

Stage or set designers should take a two- or three-year associate program at an art school or institute, or obtain a four-year bachelor of fine arts degree. Some stage designers then go on to take a two-year master's program. A good portfolio—a collection of the designer's best designs—is required for an entry-level position. On-the-job training for one to three years is recommended for beginners.

College Subjects

Art; principles of design; computer-aided design; composition of materials; fabrics and materials; color and design; sketching and drawing; two- and three-dimensional design. In addition, designers take courses in the area in which they specialize. For example, fashion designers take garment construction; furniture designers take drafting, manufacturing, and woodworking; industrial designers take mechanical and architectural drawing and structural theory; interior designers take antiques and art history; and stage and set designers take engineering and stage and set construction.

Aptitudes

Useful aptitudes for those individuals seeking a career as a designer of three-dimensional articles, products, and materials are structural visualization and memory for design.

Structural visualization, the ability to picture in one's mind the structure of three-dimensional forms, enables the designer to look at a blueprint, plan, or drawing and visualize what the finished design will look like and how the various elements of the design fit together. A stage designer, for example, can visualize from a two-dimensional plan of a theater set how the actual theater stage will look when all the design elements are in place. Similarly, a fashion designer can look at a pattern for a newly designed dress and visualize how the garment will look when it is being worn.

Memory for design is used in these professions because many designs and design elements are worked with on a daily basis. Stage designers, for example, must remember not only the overall look of a particular stage design but also the hundreds of different elements in each set.

DRAFTER

Job Description

Drafters develop detailed drawings showing the technical specifications of various kinds of manufactured products. These products range from spacecraft, automobiles, and machinery to buildings, furniture, and plumbing. Drafters take proposals that are created by scientists, engineers, designers, and architects and transform them into accurate working plans that are used to construct the product.

Drafters are classified into a number of groups according to their level of responsibility. The work of a drafter at the Drafter I level, for example, would be limited to tracing or copying finished drawings. Individuals at the Drafter V level would be expected to create unusually difficult drawings that require extensive drafting expertise.

Most drafters prepare their drawings manually, using such drafting tools as compasses, dividers, protractors, and triangles. Increasingly, however, drafters use computer-aided drafting systems (CAD) with which they prepare their drawings on the computer screen.

Most drafters work in manufacturing industries and in engineering and architectural firms. Most eventually specialize in such areas as aeronautical, architectural, automotive, electrical, electronic, marine, and mechanical drafting. Other areas of specialization include heating and ventilation systems, plumbing, tool design, and water and sewage. Patent drafters make detailed drawings of devices for which inventors are applying for patents. Civil drafters make drawings of bridges, dams, highways, breakwaters, and other civil engineering projects.

Educational Requirements

Two years of post-high school education at a technical institute or junior or community college. Training may also be obtained through three- or four-year apprenticeship programs. Individuals may also obtain training through a combination of on-the-job training and part-time schooling.

College Subjects

Blueprint drawing and reading; composition of materials; engineering drawing; industrial technology; mathematics; mechanical drawing; physical sciences; spatial organization; two- and three-dimensional design; shop skills. With the development of computer-aided drafting systems, computer science has become increasingly important.

Aptitudes

The most important aptitude for drafters is structural visualization. An individual with high structural visualization can picture in his or her mind the structure of three-dimensional forms; he can tell how something drawn as a blueprint or technical drawing will look when it is eventually built.

Today, computer-aided drafting systems are increasingly used by drafters, but conventional drafting skills are still necessary. In addition, high structural visualization is useful in mathematics, and mathematical skills are necessary in drafting.

Tweezer dexterity, an aptitude for working with small tools, is also useful to drafters, for in much of their work they use compasses, protractors, and the like. However, as more and more drafters turn to computer-aided drafting systems, tweezer dexterity will become less important.

For the most part, drafting is work of an individual nature, with the drafter sitting at his or her drafting table or in front of a computer. As a result, the person who scores subjective in personality on the word-association test—an indication that he or she prefers work of an individual nature—would be comfortable in this field.

EDITOR

Job Description

Editors plan, coordinate, and supervise the production of text and graphic materials used in publications such as magazines, books, newspapers, and trade journals. They also check the material—or have associates check it—for grammar, spelling, punctuation, and accuracy, as well as readability, style, and agreement with editorial policy.

Editors first consult with executives, department heads, and editorial staff to coordinate activities, set up production schedules, plan budgets, and formulate editorial policy. They then determine the theme of the issue and gather all related information. The editor writes or edits the material but often delegates jobs such as fact checking and research to associate or freelance editors. All material submitted by outside writers must be evaluated by the editor before publication. Editors also obtain graphic material from picture sources and assign artists and photographers to produce illustrations and photographs.

Editors organize gathered material, plan page layouts, and select type. They review final proofs and make amendments if necessary. Editors may also oversee plans of circulation or promotion personnel.

Large publications may have many editors, and their titles—such as sports editor, financial editor, or story editor—reflect their individual responsibilities.

Educational Requirements

A four-year liberal arts degree is generally required, with degrees in communications, journalism, or English preferred. An alternate course of study is through experience, which can be obtained by working as a writer or editor for a school publication or for a radio or television station as an intern.

College Subjects

English; journalism; business administration; communications; political science; sociology; psychology; publishing; history.

Aptitudes

An important aptitude for an individual seeking a career as an editor is analytical reasoning, coupled with a low or average score in structural visualization. Analytical reasoning, the ability to arrange ideas in a logical sequence, enables an editor to rework a book manuscript, a newspaper article, or a magazine article so that it has unity and coherence. A low score in structural visualization is indicative of an individual's ability to function better in the world of words than in the world of concrete things. Ideaphoria, the ability to produce a rapid flow of ideas, can also find an outlet in editing.

The field of editing has opportunities for those who score either subjective or objective in personality on the word-association test. One who scores subjective might prefer work of an individual nature, such as copyediting, which involves checking manuscripts for errors in punctuation, spelling, and grammar, or researching, which involves checking a manuscript for factual accuracy. One who scores objective, however—an indication of an ability to work compatibly with others— might prefer working as part of an editorial team. Senior editors, for example, work constantly with other people—they hire and supervise associate or assistant editors and assign topics to writers and reporters.

ENGINEER

Job Description

Engineers invent, design, develop, and produce a great variety of structures and products, from aircraft, bridges, cars, and electronic equipment to dams, engines, tunnels, and nuclear reactors.

There are four main areas of engineering: construction, machines, materials, and processes. Engineers who work in the area of construction are concerned with the planning and building of bridges, roads, dams, tunnels, and skyscrapers. Those who work in the area of materials develop, for example, new types of semiconductors, plastics, metal alloys, fuels, and other materials. Engineers who are concerned with processes help design and develop factories and systems to produce goods in new and more efficient ways. And those who work in the area of machines design not only machines but electronic devices, computers, and mechanical systems such as those used to produce electricity.

Engineers who are trained in one of these four main areas of engineering may further specialize in one of the many branches of

102

engineering. The type of work entailed in some of the main branches is detailed below.

Aerospace and *aeronautical engineers* design, develop, and help produce aircraft, missiles, and spacecraft, as well as guidance, navigation, communications, and other systems for these vehicles.

Agricultural engineers not only design farm machinery but also develop tools and systems to produce, process, and distribute agricultural products more efficiently.

Architectural engineers, working closely with architects, design and build structures and select appropriate building materials.

Biomedical engineers help develop equipment and machinery, such as CAT scans, used in hospitals and by doctors. They also design artificial organs, as well as computers for use in hospitals

Chemical engineers design the factories, as well as the processes, that produce such products as industrial chemicals, medicines, synthetic fibers, rubber, and plastics.

Civil and construction engineers design and oversee the construction of airports, buildings, tunnels, roads, dams, bridges, railroads, and water and sewage systems.

Electrical and *electronic engineers* design and develop such electrical and electronic equipment and devices as power generators, electric motors, radios, television sets, communications equipment, radar and missile guidance systems, and telephones. Those electrical engineers who specialize in the design of computers and computer systems are computer engineers.

Industrial engineers design systems used in the manufacturing of goods; they seek the most effective ways for businesses to utilize equipment, materials, energy, information, and people.

Marine engineers design ships, oil platforms, artificial islands, and offshore harbor facilities.

Mechanical engineers design power-producing or power-using machines, including internal-combustion engines, air-conditioners, heaters, robots, steam turbines, windmills, and jet engines and rockets.

Metallurgical engineers design ways to extract metals from ore, refine the metals and produce alloys.

Mining and *geological engineers* design the machinery and systems needed to discover, extract, and process minerals; they also design mines and mine transportation systems.

Nuclear engineers design and supervise the building and operation of nuclear power plants. Some also adapt radioactive materials for use in industry and medicine.

Petroleum engineers explore for new petroleum and natural gas fields, devise improved methods of refining the petroleum, and create transportation systems for petroleum products.

Educational Requirements

A four-year bachelor of science degree in engineering is required for most entry-level positions. Some engineering schools require more than a four-year bachelor degree. A number of schools have five-year programs, which consist of three years of science and two years of engineering. Others have six-year programs, which include on-the-job training. For advancement, a master of science degree and a Ph.D. are increasingly important.

College Subjects

For the first two or three years, engineering students study the basic sciences of physics, chemistry, and mathematics, as well as introductory engineering, including such subjects as engineering drawing and blueprint reading.

Beginning in their third year, they take courses in the area in which they intend to specialize. For example, civil engineers, take building design, soil mechanics, and urban planning, among other courses; electronic engineers take integrated circuits, principles of electronics, and electromagnetics; mechanical engineers take metals and alloys, industrial safety, and facilities design and materials handling; and industrial engineers take industrial plant design and business data processing.

Aptitudes

Structural visualization, the ability to picture in one's mind the structure of three-dimensional forms, is the most important aptitude for an individual seeking a career in the field of engineering. This aptitude enables the individual to look at a blueprint and visualize what the finished structure or product will look like and how the various elements of the structure or product fit together.

There are, however, a number of other useful aptitudes, depending upon the specific area of engineering being considered. Memory for design, for example, would be a helpful trait for an individual who is interested in design engineering. This field involves the application of engineering principles to the design of manufacturing facilities and such products as engines, machinery, and equipment. Similarly, if an individual has the music, or sound-related, aptitudes—tonal memory, pitch discrimination, and rhythm memory—a career in acoustical engineering would be indicated.

If an individual scores high in ideaphoria, he or she might consider sales engineering. This profession involves the selling of engineering equipment, such as industrial machinery and electric generators, and engineering services, including the training of the client's personnel and the development of new procedures.

Individuals who score either objective or subjective in personality on the word-association test will find opportunities in the field of engineering. But those who score objective—an indication that they might prefer a position that involves working with or through others, rather than one that involves working on an individual basis—might consider civil engineering. Many civil engineers work as administrators and as supervisors at construction sites for bridges, dams, airports, and the like. These positions entail considerable contact not only with clients and construction personnel but also with people in governmental regulatory agencies.

ENGINEERING TECHNICIAN

Job Description

Engineering technicians work in research and development, building or setting up equipment. They prepare and conduct experiments and assist in design work. They also prepare specifications for materials; devise and conduct quality-control tests; conduct studies for the improvement of manufacturing efficiency; and help install, operate and maintain technical equipment. For the most part, engineering technicians assist engineers and scientists. But many have their own businesses and service technical equipment at factories, plants, and other sites.

Like engineers, engineering technicians often specialize in

particular fields. The type of work entailed in some of these specialties is detailed below.

Chemical engineering technicians help chemical engineers design the factories and processes for the production of industrial chemicals, synthetic fibers, rubber, plastics, medicines, and other chemical-based products.

Civil engineering technicians assist civil engineers in the planning and construction of buildings, bridges, dams, highways, airports, tunnels, railroads, and water and sewage systems.

Electrical and *electronics engineering technician*s help design, develop, manufacture, test, service, and repair computers, radar, sonar, industrial control devices, navigational equipment, and other electrical and electronic equipment.

Industrial engineering technicians help industrial engineers design systems used in the manufacturing of goods; their goal is to develop the most efficient ways for factories, stores, repair shops, and other types of businesses to utilize equipment, materials, energy, information, and people.

Mechanical engineering technicians help mechanical engineers design and develop power-producing or power-using machines such as internal-combustion engines, jet engines and rockets, air-conditioners and heaters, robots, steam turbines, and windmills.

Educational Requirements

A minimum of an associate degree in engineering technology is required for most entry-level positions. Such degrees can be obtained at technical institutes and junior and community colleges. Many firms also hire individuals who have a bachelor's degree in engineering. In some cases, individuals with a good technical background and on-the-job training can obtain jobs as engineering technicians.

College Subjects

Engineering; physics; chemistry; mathematics; computer-aided design. In addition, engineering technicians take courses in the area in which they specialize. For example, civil engineering technicians take such courses as building design and soil mechanics; electrical and electronics engineering technicians take principles of electronics and integrated circuits; industrial engineering technicians take industrial

106

plant design; and mechanical engineering technicians take materials handling and metals and alloys.

Aptitudes
The most important aptitude for engineering technicians is structural visualization. An individual with high structural visualization can picture in his or her mind the structure of three-dimensional forms; he can tell how something drawn as a blueprint or technical drawing will look when it is eventually built. In addition, high structural visualization is useful in mathematics, and mathematical skills are essential to engineering technicians.

For the most part, the work of an engineering technician is of an individual nature, with the technician spending much of the time in a laboratory, electronics shop, industrial plant, or office. As a result, the individual who scores subjective in personality on the word-association test—an indication that he or she prefers work of an individual nature—would be comfortable in this field.

FINANCIAL MANAGER

Job Description
Financial managers oversee the flow of cash and financial instruments for many kinds of firms, such as those involved with manufacturing, finance, education, and communications. They oversee such financial functions as granting or extending lines of credit, accounting, probating estates, recording financial transactions, and administering mortgage or trust accounts. They prepare financial reports that are required by the institution to properly conduct its daily operations and to satisfy regulatory and tax requirements. Financial managers may also be in charge of promoting goodwill and generating new business, and toward this end they create and maintain relationships with the community, civic organizations, businesses, and customers.

Financial managers establish banking procedures and ensure the efficient implementation of their organization's economic and financial policies. They establish policies and make financial decisions in accordance with state and federal laws and regulations. They must keep abreast of new banking techniques and financial services, and be knowledgeable of the workings of industries allied to banking, such as real estate, insurance, and securities.

Many financial managers specialize. Some become cash managers; others, credit card operations managers; and still others, reserve officers.

Educational Requirements

A four-year bachelor's degree in business administration, accounting, or finance. Many financial management positions are filled by promoting accountants, credit analysts, loan officers, and securities analysts who prove to be proficiently skilled in their area. Many financial institutions work in cooperation with colleges and universities that offer training programs for those seeking positions as financial managers.

College Subjects

Business administration; accounting and budget management; financial analysis; data processing; corporate cash management; international banking; managerial finance; organizational behavior; economics; money and banking.

Aptitudes

If you scored high in number facility and graphoria, but not high in structural visualization, a career as a financial manager should be considered. Number facility, which measures your ability to perform arithmetic operations both quickly and accurately, would be an asset for a financial manager.

Because much of a financial manager's work involves budgeting and scheduling and requires great attention to detail, graphoria—a measure of one's speed and accuracy with paper and pencil tasks—is an important trait.

One who scores objective in personality on the word-association test would find an outlet for this characteristic as a financial manager, because the work involves working with and through many other individuals and groups. Financial managers, for example, advise businesses and individuals on financial planning, and they frequently are called upon to take part in community projects.

ILLUSTRATOR, MEDICAL AND SCIENTIFIC

Job Description

Medical and scientific illustrators create detailed drawings, paintings, diagrams, and three-dimensional models of the human body, animals, and plants. They also illustrate anatomical and pathological specimens, microorganisms, plant and animal tissue, and surgical and medical procedures. Their work is used during consultations, in exhibits, in medical textbooks and other publications, and for research and teaching activities. Medical and scientific illustrators may also develop visual aids to help in the interpretation of various kinds of research programs.

Medical and scientific illustrators work in such varied media as acrylics, oils, pencils, pen and ink, and watercolor. They also coordinate the construction of teaching models from materials such as clay, plaster, plastic, and wax. Increasingly, medical and scientific illustrators are using computer-aided design programs in their work.

Educational Requirements

There are no formal educational requirements for those seeking positions as medical and scientific illustrators. A portfolio, consisting of one's best work, is needed to apply for jobs in this profession. Assembling a portfolio requires skills that are developed in a postsecondary art school program such as a four-year bachelor's degree in applied design, graphic arts, or fine arts.

There are several ways to gain the experience necessary to obtain an entry-level job, including a two-year associate degree program or vocational education programs, but for further advancement, evidence of appropriate talent is required.

College Subjects

Art history; principles of design; designing and sketching; computer-aided design; materials; fabrics; painting; color harmony; layout; calligraphy; mathematics; anatomy; biological sciences.

Aptitudes

If you have artistic talent and knowledge of the biological sciences, you might consider a career as a medical and scientific illustrator if you scored high in structural visualization and memory for design and subjective in personality on the word-association test.

An individual with high structural visualization can picture in his mind the structure of three-dimensional forms; he can visualize the relationship between a two-dimensional technical drawing of the human heart, for example, and an actual heart. Computer-aided design is increasingly used in medical and scientific illustration, and some computer programs enable the illustrator to see his or her designs in three dimensions, but this is basically a system for making routine work easier, so high structural visualization is still a major asset.

High structural visualization is also useful for another reason: it is helpful in mathematics. Medical and scientific illustrators use mathematical skills when they work out and depict the precise sizes and proportional relationships of biological specimens.

The ability to remember designs is also a valuable trait. This aptitude helps medical and scientific illustrators to remember not only different biological specimens but also the relationships among them.

For the most part, a medical and technical illustrator sits at a drafting table or in front of a computer creating his or her detailed drawings. As a result, scoring subjective in personality on the word-association test would be helpful to those interested in the field of medical and scientific illustration, because this indicates a preference for working as an individual rather than as a member of a group.

INDUSTRIAL PRODUCTION MANAGER

Job Description

Industrial production managers coordinate and oversee activities involved with the manufacture of a company's products. They plan and direct activities that relate to production, keeping in mind time restraints, efficiency standards, and cost factors. They establish cost controls, budget restraints, production and delivery schedules, and quality control standards. They also determine what machines will be used in the manufacturing process, the sequence of production, and if overtime will be necessary. Their main goal is to achieve a point of maximum production and efficient utilization of manpower and machinery, while remaining on schedule and within the budget.

Industrial production managers also perform such tasks as inventory control, equipment purchasing, installation and maintenance of machinery and equipment, and staffing. They also coordinate efforts with other departments, such as engineering, traffic, or sales. Finally, they evaluate product samples, make changes where necessary to improve quality and efficiency, and write reports summarizing production and product performance.

Large plants generally have more than one industrial production manager, with each responsible for a specific aspect of production— machining, assembly or finishing, for example. Industrial production managers usually report to the vice president of manufacturing or the plant manager.

Educational Requirements

A four-year bachelor's degree in industrial engineering or business administration is usually required. More sophisticated production operations may require applicants to possess a master's degree, but higher level positions can be attained through promotion. Upon hiring, the company usually enrolls the employee in a training program to acquaint him or her with the specific machinery, policies and procedures, and products and materials being used and created.

College Subjects

Business administration; production control; materials; inventory management; computer science; industrial engineering; manufacturing technology; mechanical engineering; operations research; quality control; industrial safety; systems engineering.

Aptitudes

Structural visualization, the ability to picture in one's mind the structure of three-dimensional forms, is a valuable trait for an industrial production manager. This aptitude enables the individual to look at blueprints and detailed working plans of products and visualize what the finished product will look like. Structural visualization is also important to industrial production managers when they are involved in the selection and installation of machinery and equipment for the plant.

An individual who scores objective in personality on the word-association test would find an outlet for this characteristic as an industrial production manager, because the work involves almost constant contact with many other individuals, from production workers and cost estimators, to engineers, architects, and salespersons.

INSURANCE CLAIM REPRESENTATIVE

Job Description

Insurance claim representatives, who are also called insurance claim approvers, investigate insurance claims, negotiate settlements with claimants, and authorize insurance payments.

A claim representative can be either a claim adjuster or a claim examiner. For the most part, adjusters work in an office, where they review reports, police and hospital records, and the testimony of witnesses. They may also interview claimants and witnesses. In addition, they examine physical evidence prior to settling a claim. Examiners generally work in the field. They operate much like police investigators, investigating questionable claims, including those that seek unreasonable amounts of money.

When a claim adjuster receives a claim for damage or a loss from a policyholder, he or she first must determine whether the policy covers the loss. The amount of the loss must also be determined. Once it is determined that the insurance company is liable, the claim representative negotiates with the claimant to settle the case.

Some claim representatives work in all areas of insurance. Many others specialize in such areas as workers' compensation, fire damage, or product liability. Those who specialize in life and health insurance are called claim examiners.

Educational Requirements

For the most part, insurance companies prefer to hire individuals who are college graduates for the position of insurance claim representative. There are exceptions, however. An individual with specialized experience—someone who has worked in or has knowledge of the workings of an auto body shop, for example—might find employment as an insurance claim representative even if he or she has no college degree.

While some insurance companies prefer individuals with degrees in economics or business, others also seek those with liberal arts degrees. Even a degree—or at least some courses—in engineering would be an asset for an individual who seeks a career as a claim representative who deals with industrial claims.

Many big insurance companies provide beginning insurance claim representatives with on-the-job training. In addition, the Insurance Institute of America (IIA) offers educational programs dealing with property-liability insurance, and the International Claim Association (ICA) offers educational programs in life and health insurance claims administration. Both the IIA and ICA courses lead to professional certification. In most states, claim adjusters must be licensed.

Claims representatives must be knowledgeable about federal and state insurance laws and regulations. In addition, they must be able to work with computers, because claims and records are now kept almost exclusively on computers.

College Subjects

Accounting; business; computer science; business data processing; insurance; economics. In addition, insurance claim representatives should take courses in those areas in which they specialize. For example, an individual who is interested in product liability and workers' compensation insurance cases would benefit from a variety of law courses related to those areas.

Aptitudes

If you scored high in number facility and graphoria, but not high in structural visualization, you might consider a career as an insurance claim representative. Number facility, the ability to perform arithmetic operations both quickly and accurately, is certainly an asset for an insurance claims representative, as is graphoria—speed and accuracy with paper and pencil tasks.

Insurance claim representatives deal with claimants as well as with their own subordinates and superiors. They also interview witnesses, and are sometimes called upon to testify in court proceedings. As a result, a score in structural visualization that is not high is an asset, especially for those who are adjustors, because this indicates that the individual is more comfortable dealing with intangibles than with concrete things.

JOURNALIST

Job Description
Journalists collect, analyze, interpret, and report on facts, personalities, and local, state, national, and international events. Those journalists who take photographs to accompany a news story are called photojournalists. Journalists work for the print media—newspapers and magazines—and for the broadcast, or electronic, media—radio and television.

Journalists gather and verify factual information about a story through research, interviews, and observation. They then organize the material, determine its focus or emphasis, and write the story. Broadcast journalists may appear on television or radio when conducting taped or live interviews or narration. They may also report their story "live" from the scene of a newsworthy event such as a political rally. Print journalists are employed by newspapers, magazines, and press services in cities and towns of all sizes. Some are stationed in large American cities as well as in foreign countries to prepare stories on major events happening at these locations. Journalists may be assigned to gather news originating from specific places, such as police stations, the courts, or Congress. Many journalists specialize in such areas as sports, religion, science, business, politics, the environment, or the arts.

The field of journalism offers many other opportunities, and those people who are columnists, feature writers, editors, editorial writers, and news writers are also considered journalists.

Educational Requirements
A four-year bachelor of arts degree in journalism. Most potential employers look for experience on broadcast stations, community newsletters, school newspapers, and internships with news organizations. A master's degree is required for such positions as journalism teacher, researcher, and theorist.

College Subjects
Writing; English; sociology; political science; economics; history; communications; psychology; speech; business; composition; word processing.

Aptitudes

If you possess ideaphoria, the ability to come up with a rapid flow of ideas, you would find an outlet for this trait in journalism. The journalist with high ideaphoria is the one who comes up with attention-getting ideas for stories, and with the most interesting slants to the news coverage of the more common, everyday events. Ideaphoria also comes into play when journalists interview people for stories, for they are able to come up with many interesting questions for the interviewees. High ideaphoria is also important for journalists who report "live" from the scene of a newsworthy event, because it enables them to report on the event without the use of voluminous notes.

Low structural visualization, an indication that the individual prefers working in the world of words rather than in the world of concrete things, complements ideaphoria.

Because a journalist deals constantly with government officials, business executives, entertainers, and people in all walks of life, an individual who is objective in personality—an indication of an ability to work compatibly with and through others—will find an outlet for his or her personality in this field. Indeed, most journalists score objective in personality on the word-association test. There are, however, opportunities for those who are subjective in personality, as well. Subjective people—individuals who are more comfortable working as an individual rather than in a group situation—would probably be better suited to the research and writing of background articles or editorials for the news media, positions that do not demand as much interaction with the public.

LAWYER

Job Description

Lawyers advise clients of their legal rights and obligations. At times, they may also represent the client in court in civil or criminal actions, or in actions before governmental agencies. Lawyers also negotiate out-of-court settlements. In addition, they may serve as guardians, trustees, or executors.

Most lawyers are employed by law firms. Others work for businesses, the government, and private organizations. In representing a client, lawyers conduct in-depth research into applicable laws and judicial decisions that involve situations similar to those currently faced by the client. While lawyers still use law libraries when preparing cases, they increasingly supplement their research with computers that search the legal literature and identify legal texts that may be relevant.

Lawyers may specialize in one of the many areas of the legal profession. The type of work entailed in some of these areas is detailed below.

Criminal lawyers act as prosecutors or defense attorneys in law cases dealing with such criminal offenses as murder, rape, conspiracy, and theft. Prosecutors usually work in public service in a district attorney's office, and are responsible for prosecuting criminals. Defense attorneys, who have private practices, defend their clients by preparing legal documents and by representing them in litigation.

Patent lawyers advise inventors, manufacturers, and other interested individuals about patents. Their advice may have to do with the patentability of an invention, the validity of patents, or patent infringement of patents. In court cases, patent lawyers defend their clients in patent-infringement litigation or prosecute those individuals who have infringed their client's patents. Patent lawyers may also represent their clients before various administrative agencies of the federal government.

Tax lawyers advise individuals and businesses and other organizations about their legal rights and obligations with regard to estate, excise, gift, income, property, and other local, state, foreign, and federal taxes. They formulate their client's defense or initiate legal action for their client by preparing legal documents and representing the client in tax litigation in court or before administrative agencies of the government.

Other areas of specialty include divorce law, corporate law, labor law, banking and business law, insurance law, land and probate law, real estate law, maritime (or admiralty) law, and international law.

Educational Requirements

A four-year bachelor's degree, including above average undergraduate grades, prior work experience, and completion of the Law School Admission Test is required for entrance into a law school.

Completion of a three-year program in a law school accredited by the American Bar Association qualifies potential practicing lawyers for the bar examination.

There is no nationwide bar examination, and state examinations vary. Most states require applicants to take the six-hour Multistate Bar Examination (MBE); in addition, other states require the three-hour Multistate Essay Examination (MSEE) or the Multistate Professional Responsibility Examination (MPRE). This must be passed, along with an ethical examination, in order to practice law in the courts.

College Subjects

Undergraduate college students who plan to go on to law school often take what is called a "pre-law" major, but this course of studies varies with the individual and with the college. Law schools prefer those students who majored in social science, natural science, or the humanities, and whose course work included English, public speaking, history, government, economics, philosophy, mathematics, computer science, and a foreign language.

For approximately the first half of the three-year law-school program, students take such basic courses as constitutional law, judicial procedures, legal writing, contracts, property law, and torts. Thereafter, they can take courses in that area of law in which they intend to specialize.

Aptitudes

Common to all areas of law is the fact that the lawyer's primary work involves the interpretation of the law and its application to specific situations. Yet law encompasses so many specialties, and entails such a great variety of work, there are interesting opportunities for individuals with differing interests and aptitudes.

You might, for example, consider a career in law if you scored high in inductive reasoning but not high in structural visualization. Inductive reasoning is the ability to reason from the particular to the general and to form a conclusion. This trait, which enables a lawyer to see relationships or to grasp a pattern, is particularly useful to trial lawyers. A prosecuting attorney, for example, might have many bits of seemingly unrelated evidence, yet from this be able to formulate a strong case against the individual being prosecuted.

117

Low structural visualization is also helpful, because it signifies that the individual is most comfortable in a career in which words, rather than concrete things, are of importance. However, for an individual who specializes in patent law and therefore deals with blueprints and plans of three-dimensional objects, a high score in structural visualization would be useful.

Many areas of the legal profession, including trial law and the teaching of law in colleges and universities, also offer an excellent outlet for ideaphoria, the ability to come up with a rapid flow of ideas. Trial lawyers, especially, must have the ability to speak persuasively. This is true whether they represent their clients in a criminal court or before a government regulatory agency.

Ideaphoria is also useful to those lawyers who work in government as legislative aides and counsels, because they are often responsible not only for drafting legislation but for influencing those legislators who will later vote on the legislation.

An objective score in personality on the word-association test would also be useful in this field, because an objective score indicates an ability to work well with and through other people. On the other hand, an individual who scored subjective in personality would be more at home working behind the scenes preparing the legislation.

Because much of a lawyer's work involves research and writing and requires great attention to detail, graphoria—the test in visual perception that measures your speed and accuracy with paper and pencil tasks—is also an asset.

In some specialized areas of the legal profession, other aptitudes may come into play. For example, a lawyer with the auditory, or sound-related, aptitudes—tonal memory, pitch discrimination, and rhythm memory—could derive greater satisfaction if he or she practiced in the area of entertainment law.

LIBRARIAN

Job Description
Librarians collect, organize, catalog, and lend books, films, computer tapes, periodicals, clippings, and records and tapes to those who require their use. They maintain library collections and assist

individuals and organizations in locating and utilizing information. Librarians also furnish information regarding library rules, activities, and services.

Librarians supervise the issuing and receiving of materials for circulation or for use in the library. They also answer correspondence on special reference subjects. Librarians may also coordinate projects involving promotion of library activities. In addition, librarians may also review published and unpublished material, prepare bibliographies, and advise individuals and organizations on information sources. In small libraries, librarians handle all aspects of work, including budget preparation and the supervision of other administrative services. In large libraries, librarians may specialize in such areas as reference, music, art, special collections, cataloging, classifying, or acquisitions. Many librarians specialize in children's and young-adult collections.

Most librarians work in school libraries, public libraries, or libraries in institutions of higher education. Some work for business or law firms, historical societies, newspapers, labor unions, movie studios, government agencies, or other organizations that possess their own libraries.

Educational Requirements

A four-year bachelor of arts degree in library science with courses in education or the equivalent in education and work experience. For most positions, a master's degree in library science is required. In most states, school librarians must be trained and certified not only as librarians but also as teachers. Librarians who specialize in a particular area—art, for example—must have a master's degree or a Ph.D. in that field of interest.

College Subjects

Library science; education; literature; history of books and printing; science; censorship; English; bookkeeping; business; computers; subjects in field of interest or specialization.

Aptitudes

If you are high in graphoria but low or average in structural visualization, you might consider a career as a librarian. Speed and accuracy with paper and pencil tasks (high graphoria), as measured by the number-checking test, is an important aptitude for librarians, because their tasks often involve cataloging, classifying, budgeting, and other types of paper work. Being low or average in structural visualization is also important, because it indicates that you are more at home in the world of words than in the world of concrete things.

If you have a good memory, you will find an outlet for this trait as a librarian, because it is helpful to be able to remember titles and authors of books. High number memory is especially helpful in remembering a book's Dewey Decimal or other classification number.

Ideaphoria—the ability to produce a rapid flow of ideas—is another aptitude that is usable by some librarians, especially school librarians, who often have to think of ways to get children and young adults interested in various subjects or to get them to give up other Saturday activities and come to the library.

In addition to those aptitudes mentioned above, there are aptitudes that would be of benefit to those individuals seeking a career as special librarians. The auditory, or sound-related, aptitudes, for example, would benefit a music librarian, and memory for design would be helpful to an art librarian.

There are many different aspects to library work, so individuals who score either objective or subjective in personality on the word-association test can do well in this field. A person who scores objective might prefer working with the general public, helping people learn how to use the library. An objective personality is especially important for children's librarians, because they often conduct or supervise story hours. If you scored subjective, however—an indication that you might prefer working as an individual rather than as part of a team or with groups of people—you might be more at home doing such necessary tasks as cataloging, classifying, budgeting, or acquisition work.

MANAGER, GENERAL

Job Description

General managers plan, organize, direct, control, and coordinate the operations of an organization or its major departments. They often do this in collaboration with other company officers and the board of directors. Depending on the size of the organization, they may report to a chief executive officer, chief operating officer, or an executive vice president.

General managers direct their organization's or department's activities within the framework of the organization's overall plan. With the help of supervisory managers and their staffs, they strive to achieve their department's goals as rapidly and economically as possible.

General managers work in almost every industry. The types of work entailed in four of these industries is detailed below.

Education administrators provide leadership and coordinate the day-to-day management of educational activities in colleges, universities, and schools. They set up and implement operational policies, programs, and goals. School principals, assistant principals, deans of students, financial aid directors, and registrars are among the many kinds of education administrators.

Health-services managers plan, organize, coordinate, and supervise the delivery of health care. They include generalists, such as administrators of hospitals, nursing homes, and other health-care facilities, and specialists, such as managers of specific clinical departments or services.

Hotel managers operate hotels and motels. They set room rates, manage the housekeeping, maintenance, and accounting departments, and oversee the dining room and kitchen staffs.

Restaurant and food-service managers operate restaurants and institutional food-service facilities. They are responsible for the selection and pricing of items on the menu, the quality of the food and service, and the efficient use of food and labor, as well as a variety of administrative functions.

Other general management positions include personnel manager, store manager, and brokerage office manager.

Educational Requirements

Because their career fields and responsibilities are so diverse, the educational requirements of general managers are also varied. Most organizations, however, require at least a bachelor's degree in business administration, liberal arts, or science. Many individuals who aspire to become general managers and administrators go on to attain a master's degree or a Ph.D.

An individual's major field of concentration in college should be related to that career area he or she expects to enter. For example, an individual who wants to become a general manager of a social-services agency should major in sociology. Similarly, those seeking to rise to the top in hospital administration should obtain a master's degree in health-service administration or nursing administration, and those who want to become general managers in the field of education should pursue a doctorate in education administration. Degrees are offered in many colleges and universities in the fields of hotel management and restaurant and food-service management.

General managers and executives, whatever their educational achievements, usually must work their way up in an organization by displaying leadership qualities.

College Subjects

General managers constantly deal with many people, so they must have highly developed personal skills. Therefore, courses in written and oral communication are important, as are courses in sociology and psychology. And because so much of their work is administrative, courses in business management, accounting, and economics are also important. In addition, courses specific to the individual's particular field of endeavor should be taken, as indicated below.

Education administrator: school management; school finance and budgeting; school law; curriculum development and evaluation; community relations; politics in education; personnel administration.

Health-services administrator: health-care policy; hospital organization and management; medical care administration; health administration; budget control; personnel administration; health information systems management.

Hotel managers: hotel administration; marketing; housekeeping; food-service management and catering; hotel maintenance; engineering; data processing.

Restaurant and food-service managers: business law and management; food planning and preparation; nutrition.

Aptitudes

An objective personality suggests management. In addition, a characteristic of top managers is a large English vocabulary. Major executives score higher on the English vocabulary test than every other group, including writers. The reason for this is that words are the tools of thought. People think with words. They use them to express themselves. They use them to put across ideas. In no area of the world of work are words more important than in management positions, because managers must be able to communicate clearly, both orally and in writing. They must be able to use these words to motivate those who work for them, and to display and express a self-confidence to those they report to.

An individual who scores objective in personality on the word-association test would find an outlet for this characteristic as a manager, because the work involves almost constant contact with many other individuals, from subordinates to members of the organization's board of directors. There are, however, also opportunities for those who are subjective in personality, an indication that they would be more comfortable working as an individual. They would be comfortable in a position where specialized knowledge is important, such as managing an antique shop or some other small specialty business.

There are also many opportunities in general management for individuals who score either high or low in ideaphoria. Those who score high—an indication that they can come up with a rapid flow of ideas—would probably be better suited to managing some kind of small business. Their responsibilities and activities would be much like those of an entrepreneur who develops his or her own business: Success depends upon a steady stream of ideas to get the business off the ground and to keep it growing. Low ideaphoria, on the other hand, would be an asset for the general manager of a large business. In this situation, the ability to keep the enterprise running smoothly and efficiently is more important than the ability to come up with a rapid flow of ideas.

Because general managers work in such a wide variety of businesses, other aptitudes may also come into play. For example, the music aptitudes—tonal memory, pitch discrimination, and rhythm memory—would be assets for those individuals seeking a career as the general manager of a concert hall or orchestra. And memory for design would be an asset for those seeking a career as the general manager of an art gallery or as the curator of a museum.

MARKETING MANAGER

Job Description

A marketing manager develops a company's overall marketing plan for its products or services. Marketing entails the following: determining the demand for the company's products and services; identifying potential customers, such as businesses, wholesalers, retailers, the general public, and government agencies; developing pricing strategies; and promoting and distributing the product. The basic goal of a marketing manager is to maximize consumer satisfaction with his company's products and thus maximize profitability.

Because of the broad scope of activities involved in marketing, marketing managers work closely with managers of other departments. They work with product-development managers in the creation of new products or the improvement of existing ones. They work with sales-promotion and advertising managers to promote and describe the firm's products and services in the best possible way and to attract and sway potential users. And they work with market-research managers to identify potential customers so as to increase the firm's share of the market and ultimately its profits. Marketing managers also coordinate efforts to monitor consumer trends regarding services and products.

Educational Requirements

A bachelor's or master's degree in business administration, with the emphasis on marketing, and marketing experience. Many employers also accept applicants with a bachelor's degree in psychology, sociology, literature, or other liberal arts subjects.

College Subjects

Advertising; marketing communications; computers; business law; English; economics; finance; statistics; psychology; accounting; product management; sociology; international marketing; market research; demography.

Aptitudes

Ideaphoria, the ability to come up with a rapid flow of ideas, is a useful aptitude for marketing managers because the individual must have the ability to come up with ideas for the development and marketing of new products, and for planning new ways to market old products. Marketing managers must understand why customers and consumers make the choices they do, and they must be able to communicate this information to the rest of the marketing staff. They also must be able to spot new trends and devise new product-distribution methods, and be able to communicate this information to the staff.

Marketing managers must be completely familiar with the company's products or services, as well as with the promotional tools used to market those products or services. For those who work for companies that manufacture and market such products as computers, electronic equipment, machinery, and the like, high structural visualization is an important asset. For those who work for firms that market services or non-three-dimensional products—magazines, for example—low structural visualization would be an asset.

Many marketing managers work daily with advertising and sales promotion managers, as well as with customers and consumers. And at many small companies, marketing managers also serve as sales managers, and are thus responsible for the direction of the sales staff. As a result, this field offers many opportunities for those individuals who score objective in personality on the word-association test—an indication that the individual prefers working with or through other people. There are, however, also opportunities in the marketing field for those who score subjective, an indication that they might prefer working as an individual. Such individuals might, for example, be responsible for the development of various kinds of marketing displays.

NURSE, REGISTERED

Job Description

Registered nurses provide general nursing care to patients in hospitals, infirmaries, sanitariums, or similar institutions. Nurses take temperature, blood pressure, pulse, and other vital signs. They determine patients' progress, record significant conditions and reactions to detect deviations from normal, and administer medication prescribed by physicians. Nurses also assist in rehabilitation and instruct patients and their families in proper care.

The largest group of registered nurses is employed in hospitals. Most are staff nurses who provide bedside nursing care and carry out the medical regimen prescribed by physicians. Some hospital nurses may work in the operating room; some may work with the aged or with cancer patients. Other nurses work in nursing homes, where they care for residents with conditions ranging from a broken bone to Parkinson's disease.

Public health nurses care for patients in schools, health agencies, and other community settings. Office nurses are employed by physicians in private practice, clinics, and health maintenance organizations. Occupational health or industrial nurses provide care to employees in industry and government. Private duty nurses tend to patients at home or in hospitals who need constant care.

Many registered nurses specialize: some become anesthetists; some supervisors or administrators; and others, practitioners in such areas as intensive care, pediatric nursing, or geriatric care.

Educational Requirements

There are three major educational paths to becoming a registered nurse: associate degree, diploma, and bachelor of science degree in nursing. Associate degree programs are offered by community and junior colleges and take about 2 years. Diploma programs are given at hospitals and last 2 to 3 years. Bachelor of science degrees in nursing are offered at colleges and universities and require 4 to 5 years. All states require that a practicing registered nurse be licensed. A license is obtained by completing one of the aforementioned programs and by passing a national examination administered by each state.

College Subjects

Anatomy; chemistry; drug calculations; microbiology; nutrition; obstetrics; physiology; psychiatric nursing; psychology and other behavioral sciences.

Aptitudes

High graphoria—speed and accuracy with paper and pencil tasks—is an important aptitude for nurses because they spend a substantial amount of time keeping records and writing reports. They test for and record the patients' vital signs, including blood pressure, heart rate, pulse rate, and temperature. And they report on everything that is done to their patients, including medication and treatments, and how the patients responded.

Tweezer dexterity is another important aptitude for nurses, because they must be adept at handling hypodermic needles, catheters, hemostats (clamps), and other small instruments and tools. Often, nurses use tweezers to remove sutures (stitches), and operating room nurses are called upon to suture incisions.

There are many different aspects to the nursing profession, so individuals who are either objective or subjective in personality can do well in this field. Those who are objective—an indication that they might prefer working as part of a health-care team or with groups of people—would be comfortable working with groups of patients and instructing patients and their families about proper health care. Such individuals could also advance to the position of head nurse and then to management-level nursing. In nursing homes, for example, registered nurses often supervise licensed practical nurses, an activity suitable to those who are objective in personality. An objective personality would also be an asset to public health nurses, who work with community leaders, teachers, and parents, and also instruct community groups in matters relating to health. If you are subjective, however—an indication that you might prefer working as an individual rather than as part of a team or with groups of people—you might be more at home as a private duty nurse, working with individual patients at home, in a hospital, or in a nursing home. A subjective personality might also be advantageous to nurses who work for a doctor in his or her office.

OCCUPATIONAL THERAPIST

Job Description

Occupational therapists help people who are physically or psychologically impaired as a result of mental illness, disease, injuries, disabilities, or aging. Through therapy, they help their patients regain control over their lives.

Occupational therapists first record the patient's medical history. They then evaluate his or her physical ability by conducting a series of tests that measure muscular strength, motor coordination, hearing, and sight. They may also evaluate the patient's ability to work and communicate with others. Then, working with a physician, vocational counselor, and other health-care professionals, as well as with the patient's family, they develop a therapy plan for the patient. The plan may include vocational, educational, and recreational activities whose purpose is to help the patient become self-sufficient.

For those who are suffering from some form of mental illness, the therapy may include the teaching of communication skills, and helping the patient to develop motivation and concentration. For those who are physically impaired, the therapist will work on improving their strength, endurance, and motor skills. In some cases, the therapist may have to help the patient learn or relearn such basic skills as dressing and cooking. In other cases, the therapist will teach the patient such crafts as jewelry-making, weaving, and leather-working, as well as such practical needs as typing and the use of tools. When working with children, the therapist may work with toys and games.

Because of these practical applications, occupational therapy programs are often described as "curing by doing." The patient is continually monitored, and over time, as the patient improves, the treatments may be changed to reflect that improvement.

Occupational therapists work in hospitals, clinics, nursing homes, rehabilitation centers, homes, schools, day-care centers, and factories. Some work for home health agencies, camps for the handicapped, and public health departments. Many establish their own private practices.

Though many occupational therapists treat a wide variety of mental and physical illnesses, the field is becoming increasingly specialized, with practitioners concentrating on the aged, children, the mentally disabled, or those suffering injuries.

Educational Requirements

The minimum educational requirement for an occupational therapist is a bachelor's degree in occupational therapy, though a postbaccalaureate degree is increasingly important, especially for those who expect to teach, do research, or enter into administration. To obtain a license as a registered occupational therapist in most states, an individual must also have six to nine months of clinical experience in a hospital and pass an examination administered by the American Occupational Therapy Certification Board.

Individuals who have completed high school and who have completed a course of studies in occupational therapy can receive a diploma as a certified occupational therapy assistant.

College Subjects

Anatomy; art; biology; chemistry; health; crafts; human growth and development; physics; psychology; psychology of the handicapped; physiology.

Aptitudes

Occupational therapists will find a number of aptitudes helpful. Among them is ideaphoria, the ability to produce a rapid flow of ideas, because occupational therapy is an intensely people-oriented profession that requires constant communication between the therapist and the patient. The therapist who is able to produce lots of ideas that are useful in therapy will be better able to help the patient overcome his or her disability. Ideaphoria is especially important to those occupational therapists who teach the subject.

If you possess finger or tweezer dexterity, you will find an outlet for these traits because occupational therapists often work with small tools when teaching patients about jewelry-making, weaving, and other crafts.

Because occupational therapists often need to design or make special equipment for patients to use at home or at work, an average or high score in structural visualization is an asset. Occupational therapists often work with engineers to develop devices, for example, that enable a handicapped patient to operate a television set, a phone, or some other device.

OFFICE MANAGER

Job Description

Office managers supervise and coordinate the activities of clerical departments and their personnel in various organizations. In order to ensure efficient operation, they monitor and evaluate all aspects of office operations and procedures, including clerical support, equipment and machinery maintenance, bookkeeping, and payroll preparation.

As part of their job, office managers recruit, interview and make recommendations about hiring personnel. They also train new employees, familiarizing them, for example, with the office's computer systems and showing them how to use new software. Their duties also include supply requisition, correspondence flow, and overseeing the cataloging, storage, retrieval and disposal of office records.

Office managers allocate responsibilities to subordinates and determine ways to carry out these responsibilities more efficiently. They also prepare employee evaluations, benefits, and insurance packages, and they approve requests for vacations and overtime. As liaison between clerical personnel and managerial staff, office managers must keep their superiors informed about the efficiency of the office as well as listen to complaints and suggestions made by subordinates.

Educational Requirements

A two-year associate degree is required by some employers; others seek individuals with a bachelor's degree. Most office managers, however, have been supervisors in other organizations, or have been promoted from within the organization. Mastery of office equipment, the ability to communicate effectively with other workers, and the ability to organize and coordinate responsibilities efficiently are attributes that superiors look for, and are more important than a degree.

College Subjects

Computer organization and programming; purchasing; business administration; managerial accounting; organizational behavior; auditing concepts; managerial finance; interpersonal communication; information science; business data processing.

Aptitudes

If you scored high in graphoria but not high in structural visualization, and if you are objective in personality as determined by the word-association test, you might consider a career as an office manager.

Despite the fact that office and clerical work is becoming increasingly computerized, graphoria—speed and accuracy with paper and pencil tasks—is still an important aptitude for office managers, because much preliminary work—the writing of drafts of reports, for example—may be done with paper and pencil prior to the keyboarding of the material. Graphoria also comes into play when the office manager reviews reports and records prepared by subordinates.

Office managers must be in constant communication not only with their subordinates, but with their superiors. They interview prospective employees, train them after they are hired, and plan, oversee, and evaluate their work. In addition, they coordinate meetings, deal with labor-management problems, and keep their supervisors informed of progress and problems. As a result, low structural visualization—an indication that the individual is more comfortable in the world of words than in the world of concrete things—is a major asset for office managers, as is an objective personality—an indication that the individual can work well with and through other people.

PHYSICIAN

Job Description

Physicians perform medical examinations, diagnose diseases, treat people who are ill due to injury or disease, and advise families and patients on self-care to prevent illness. Many physicians also do research into the causes, transmission, and control of disease.

There are two types of physicians: doctor of medicine and doctor of osteopathy. Both schools of medicine may use all accepted methods of treatment, including drugs and surgery. However, doctors of osteopathy, who believe that good health requires the proper alignment of bones, ligaments, muscles, and nerves, place emphasis on the body's musculoskeletal system. Physicians diagnose and treat patients in private offices or in hospitals. They may also visit patients at home if necessary.

Most physicians provide patient care and have office practices, although some work as residents or are full-time staff members in hospitals. Others teach or become researchers and administrators. Some physicians are general practitioners but most specialize in one of the many branches of medicine. The type of work entailed in some of medicine's main branches is detailed below.

Allergists and *immunologists* diagnose and treat diseases and conditions that are caused by allergic or immunological factors.

Anesthesiologists administer anesthetics to patients during surgery and other medical procedures to induce unconsciousness, or to induce general or local insensitivity to pain

Cardiologists diagnose and treat diseases of the heart and the blood vessels.

Dermatologists diagnose and treat diseases of the human skin.

Endocrinologists diagnose and treat diseases of the endocrine glands and the hormones associated with them.

Gastroenterologists treat and diagnose diseases of the stomach and intestines.

Gynecologists diagnose and treat diseases and disorders of the female genital, urinary, and rectal organs.

Internists diagnose and treat diseases and injuries of human internal organ systems. Internal medicine has a number of subspecialties, including cardiology, gastroenterology, nephrology, pulmonary disorders, rheumatology, infectious diseases, and endocrinology.

Nephrologists diagnose and treat diseases of the kidneys.

Neurologists diagnose and treat organic diseases and disorders of the nervous system.

Obstetricians treat women during the prenatal, natal, and postnatal periods.

Ophthalmologists diagnose and treat diseases and injuries of the eyes.

Orthopedists diagnose and treat diseases and disorders of the bones, joints, muscles, extremities, and spine.

Otolaryngologists diagnose and treat diseases of the ear, nose, and throat.

Pathologists study the nature, causes, and development of diseases, and the structural and functional changes caused by them.

Pediatricians care for and diagnose and treat diseases of infants and children.

Plastic surgeons surgically treat the skin and face for reconstructive or cosmetic purposes.

Psychiatrists study, diagnose, and treat mental, emotional. and behavioral disorders.

Radiologists diagnose and treat diseases of the human body, using X-rays and radioactive substances.

Rheumatologists diagnose and treat diseases of the joints.

Surgeons perform surgery to correct deformities, repair injuries, prevent diseases, and improve functions in patients. Like nonsurgical physicians, surgeons often specialize in such areas as neurology, obstetrics/gynecology, ophthalmology, orthopedic surgery, otolaryngology, plastic surgery, and urology.

Urologists diagnose and treat diseases and disorders of the genital and urinary organs and the genitourinary tract.

Educational Requirements

A four-year bachelor of arts or science degree and a four-year doctor of medicine degree. All states require that physicians be licensed. Licensed physicians must be graduated from an accredited professional school, complete a one- to six-year internship/residency program after graduation, and pass a licensing examination administered by the National Board of Medical Examiners or the National Board of Osteopathic Medical Examiners. Specialists must complete two to four years in advanced residency training, followed by two or more years of practice in the specialty. They must also pass examinations in their specialty.

College Subjects

Pre-med and medical-school courses include biology; physics; inorganic and organic chemistry; mathematics; anatomy; physiology; pharmacology; microbiology; pathology; biochemistry.

Aptitudes

An important aptitude for physicians is structural visualization, the ability to visualize solids. This trait is important for the study of anatomy, and it is vital for surgeons, who must know exactly where— and how deep—to make their incisions during an operation.

Inductive reasoning, the ability to reason from the particular to the general and to form a conclusion, would seem to find an outlet in diagnostic medicine. This aptitude is what enables the physician to recognize a patient's symptoms, interpret the results of laboratory tests, and make a diagnosis that leads to a proper course of treatment.

Ideaphoria, the ability to come up with a rapid flow of ideas, is usable in some areas of medical practice. High ideaphoria is useful, for example, to psychiatrists, because it enables them be more effective in helping patients with their problems. Ideaphoria is also helpful to a physician who teaches the subject, because it enables him or her to present the subject in a clear and interesting way. Similarly, physicians working in the area of public health, which involves the education of the general public, will also find ideaphoria useful.

PROPERTY MANAGER

Job Description

Property managers supervise the day-to-day management of buildings such as apartment houses, retail and industrial properties, condominiums, and office buildings. They coordinate the activities of workers who install, operate, and maintain facilities and equipment in such buildings. They work either for real-estate management companies or as independent managers.

Property managers usually manage a number of properties at the same time. Their responsibilities are quite varied and include setting the rental or leasing rates, advertising for tenants when there is vacant space, negotiating rental contracts, and collecting rent payments from tenants. They also oversee personnel who prepare financial statements for the properties and keep records of rents due and other accounts receivable, as well as records showing disbursement of payments for taxes, insurance, mortgages, payroll, and maintenance costs.

Property managers keep building owners abreast of the status of the property by submitting statements regarding lease expiration dates, occupancy rates, and problems with tenants. They negotiate and authorize contracts for services such as grounds-keeping, security, trash removal, and repair. And they evaluate the workers' performance and supervise the purchasing of equipment and supplies.

Some property managers, called resident managers, work on-site. Others employ building engineers who hire on-site management personnel to handle daily activities.

Educational Requirements

A college degree in business administration, real estate, finance, or public administration is usually required. Experience is obtained by working as a property manager's assistant or as a real-estate agent. Property managers usually begin by managing a small apartment complex. With experience, they may assume more responsibility and handle larger properties or several properties at once.

College Subjects

Finance; business administration; real estate; advertising; business management; marketing; building maintenance; business and real-estate law; insurance and risk management; accounting.

Aptitudes

If you scored high in graphoria and objective in personality, you might find an outlet for these traits as a property manager.

Graphoria—speed and accuracy with paper and pencil tasks—is an important aptitude for property managers because much of their work involves the compilation and keeping of such records as rents due, taxes, mortgages, maintenance costs, payroll, and insurance. They also submit periodic reports to building owners, keeping them abreast of ongoing operations and problems, and prepare financial statements, leases and other documents.

Property managers must be in constant communication not only with building owners but with maintenance workers, groundskeepers, elevator operators and a host of other individuals for whom they are directly responsible. They must also deal constantly with individuals and firms that provide supplies and equipment for the property, all of which requires both communication and administrative ability. As a result, an objective personality—an indication that you are able to work well with and through other people—would be helpful.

PSYCHOLOGIST

Job Description

Psychologists systematically study the behavior of individuals and groups. They seek to understand people's actions, how they grow and evolve, how they learn, and how and why they differ from one another. There are two major categories in the field of psychology—basic psychology and applied psychology. Psychologists who practice basic psychology do research into the various aspects of human behavior. Psychologists who practice applied psychology draw on the research of basic psychology to achieve socially useful goals. The goals include the diagnosis and treatment of people with behavior disorders, the reduction of tension between groups, and the creation of productive learning environments for students and work environments for workers.

The largest specialty within applied psychology is clinical psychology. Clinical psychologists are concerned with helping mentally or emotionally disturbed individuals adjust to life. They do this by helping them understand their problems, gain control over their problem behavior, and think and behave in new ways. Toward this end, they interview patients, give diagnostic tests, provide individual, family, and group therapy, and devise and initiate procedures for dealing with the individual's problems.

Psychologists first study the patient's medical and case history. Then they administer and evaluate achievement, intelligence, interest, personality, and other psychological tests. This helps them to diagnose the patient's disorders and to develop methods and plans of treatment. They also may consult with physicians, psychiatrists, and other specialists before determining the proper treatment.

Some psychologists work in universities, where they train graduate students. Others serve as consultants to educational, welfare, and similar agencies, where they evaluate, plan, and develop mental health programs. Still others conduct research in the fields of diagnosis, treatment, and prevention of mental disorders. Many clinical psychologists specialize in specific areas, such as crime and delinquency.

The type of work entailed in some of the areas of specialization in psychology is detailed below.

Clinical psychologists diagnose mental stress and help the mentally ill or emotionally disturbed adjust to life. They generally work in hospitals or clinics, or maintain their own practices.

Cognitive psychologists study how people receive, process, retrieve, and utilize knowledge.

Community psychologists utilize their knowledge to address problems of urban and rural life.

Comparative psychologists study and compare the behavior of human beings and animals.

Counseling psychologists help people deal with their everyday personal, social, educational, and vocational problems.

Developmental psychologists study how people's behavior changes as they grow from infancy through childhood and adolescence to maturity and old age.

Educational psychologists and *school psychologists* help devise educational programs and teaching procedures that lead to enhanced learning and also counsel students about personal as well as educational problems.

Experimental psychologists study such behavioral processes as perception, thinking, learning, memory, and motivation.

Health psychologists counsel people about health so that they can avoid serious emotional or physical illness.

Industrial psychologists utilize psychological techniques to make businesses, industries, and organizations operate more humanely and more efficiently.

Personality psychologists study human nature, differences between individuals, and the ways in which these differences develop.

Physiological psychologists study the relationships between human behavior and the biological and neurological functions of the body.

Psychometricians devise tests that measure aptitudes, competence, verbal skills, and personality.

Social psychologists study people's interactions with other individuals and with societal groups.

Other areas of specialization include consumer psychology, engineering psychology, forensic psychology, population psychology, and psychopharmacology.

Educational Requirements

A three- to four-year Ph.D. or Psy.D., in addition to serving an internship. Most states require that those who enter independent practice must meet specific certification or licensing criteria, possess a doctorate in psychology, have one to two years of professional experience, and pass a standardized test or oral examination. Some states require continuing education in order to obtain an updated license.

College Subjects

Experimental psychology; biology; zoology; sociology; humanities; statistics; mathematics; anatomy; intimate relationships; applied psychology; interpersonal communication; group therapy; psychotherapy; clinical work; courses in area of specialty.

Aptitudes

If you scored high in inductive reasoning and low or average in structural visualization, a career in psychology would give you an outlet for these traits. Inductive reasoning, the ability to reason from the particular to the general and to form a conclusion, enables the clinical psychologist, for example, to take a set of facts or observations and develop a theory that explains them; that is, to relate the client's symptoms to his or her underlying problems.

Because applied psychology is an intensely people-oriented profession, with the psychologist in constant communication with the client, this profession would giver you ample opportunity to use ideaphoria. Clearly, the psychologist who is able to produce a rapid flow of ideas will be better able to devise methods to overcome a patient's problems. Ideaphoria would also be helpful to a psychologist who teaches the subject, for it would enable him or her to present the subject matter in a clear and interesting way.

Low structural visualization would complement ideaphoria, because the possession of this trait indicates that the individual would prefer a career in which words, rather than concrete things, are at the heart of his or her work.

In some areas of basic psychology. however—experimental psychology, for example—high structural visualization, rather than low or average, would be an asset, because work in this field often entails the design and construction of laboratory equipment and testing apparatuses.

Similarly, the auditory aptitudes—tonal memory, pitch discrimination, and rhythm memory—would be useful to those psychologists who use music therapy in their treatment programs.

PUBLIC RELATIONS WORKER

Job Description
Public relations workers develop and conduct programs designed to create and maintain favorable publicity for individuals, corporations, trade groups, charitable foundations, government agencies, and other organizations. Toward this end, they research and compile information on the organization's activities, policies, and accomplishments. This information, which may be aimed at the public, the financial community, employees, customers, or legislators, is supplied free of charge to newspapers and magazines, television and radio stations, and business and trade publications. Many local newspapers and radio stations are heavily dependent on the free material supplied to them by public relations firms.

In addition to supplying printed matter, public relations workers also prepare exhibits, create films, write and deliver speeches, and engage in question-and-answer sessions. Public relations workers also oversee such public relations functions as fund-raising, interest-group representation, and political campaigns.

Some public relations workers concentrate on purchasing advertising space and time, others on researching data. Many specialize in fund-raising events.

Many public relations workers are employed by public relations firms, which charge their clients a fee. Others work in the public relations or communications departments of large corporations.

Educational Requirements
A four-year bachelor of arts degree combined with public relations experience. Experience can be obtained by writing for a school newspaper or working for a radio or television station. Appropriate majors include business, journalism, liberal arts, and public relations. Employers prefer a background consistent with their organization's activities.

College Subjects
Advertising; public relations; public speaking; communications; computers; business; English; economics; journalism; creating writing; political science; psychology; sociology.

Aptitudes

A career in public relations should provide you with an outlet for ideaphoria, the ability to come up with a rapid flow of ideas. This trait is a major asset for public relations workers, who often must write speeches, press releases, brochures, reports, pamphlets, newsletters, scripts, and other material about a wide variety of subjects. Ideaphoria also comes into play when they deal with telephone inquiries or interact with the public in other ways. Low structural visualization, an indication that the individual would prefer working in a field that involves words rather than concrete things, complements ideaphoria.

Public relations workers must motivate others, so, for the most part, they need to be outgoing and persuasive. As a result, individuals who are objective in personality—an indication of an ability to work compatibly with others—will find many opportunities in this field. There are, however, opportunities for those who are subjective in personality, as well. Subjective people—individuals who are more comfortable working as an individual rather than in a group situation—would probably be better suited to the writing aspects of public relations work.

REAL ESTATE DEVELOPER

Job Description

Real estate developers work for land development companies. They acquire parcels of land for the development and construction of houses, apartment buildings, shopping centers, malls, office buildings, or industrial parks. To eliminate obstacles to the development of the land, and to gain approval for the project, real estate developers must negotiate with local governments, community and public interest groups, and representatives of public utilities. It sometimes takes developers years to win approval for a project, particularly if it is a large one.

Once approval for the project is obtained, developers negotiate loans to finance the construction of the project. They then contract with architectural firms to draw up detailed plans, and with construction companies to build the project. When the project is at or near completion, they negotiate mortgage loans.

Educational Requirements

A college degree in business administration, real estate, finance, or public administration is usually required, although some companies accept individuals with liberal arts degrees. Experience can be obtained through employment as a real estate developer's assistant or in related real estate positions. Real estate developers must also have considerable knowledge about state and local laws governing land development.

College Subjects

Finance; business administration; real estate; business management; marketing; business and real-estate law; environmental law; insurance and risk management; accounting.

Aptitudes

The Foundation believes that ideaphoria and structural visualization can be used in the field of real estate development. Ideaphoria, the ability to produce a rapid flow of ideas, enables the individual to be creative in the way he or she brings a project to fruition. Ideaphoria also helps the developer in his or her role as a salesperson—a role that entails convincing state and local officials, as well as others, that the project would, for example, benefit the community while not being harmful to the environment.

High structural visualization, the ability to picture in one's mind the structure of three-dimensional forms, is of great importance to developers. The high structure developer who has learned to read blueprints and building plans can look at them and visualize what the finished project will look like and how the various structures in the project fit together. He is also better able to work intelligently with the high structure architects and construction managers who design and build the project.

Real estate developers must interact constantly with a host of individuals, including city planners, architects, engineers, construction supervisors, and county, city, town, and village officials. As a result, an objective score in personality on the word association test is important, because this indicates an ability to function well in—and to enjoy—a career that involves almost constant interaction with a variety of people.

SALESPERSON

Job Description

There are 15 million salespeople in the United States who sell products and services to individuals, retail and wholesale establishments, manufacturers, government agencies, associations, and other businesses and organizations. The products they sell range from books, clothing, furniture, and processed foods to industrial equipment, pharmaceutical supplies, toys, and computers. The services range from insurance, real estate, and printing to advertising, financial services, and utilities.

Salespeople who work in retail stores, as well as door-to-door salespeople, sell merchandise directly to the public. Wholesale salespeople sell merchandise to retailers, commercial companies, institutions, schools, and hospitals. Salespeople not only sell products and services but also are responsible for winning new customers and for creating goodwill.

Some salespeople receive a salary, but most work on a commission, receiving money for each product or service sold.

The type of work entailed in various types of selling jobs is detailed below.

Retail sales workers are employed by stores and showrooms to help customers select and purchase consumer goods. The depth of knowledge required of retail salespeople is determined by the product being sold. An automobile salesperson, for example, would have to have substantial knowledge about the workings of a car.

Manufacturers' representatives and *wholesale sales representatives* sell their company's products to other manufacturers, wholesale establishments, retail stores, government agencies, and other institutions. In their work, which often involves a substantial amount of traveling, they show samples, pictures, and catalogs to prospective buyers.

Insurance sales workers, who are also called agents or brokers, sell life, health, automobile, home, accident, fire and theft, and other insurance policies to individuals and companies.

Securities sales workers buy and sell stocks and bonds, shares in mutual funds, certificates of deposit, insurance annuities, and other financial products for individuals and organizations.

142

Financial services sales representatives, who usually work for banks and savings and loan institutions, solicit applications for loans, new deposit accounts, and other financial services from individuals and business establishments.

Real estate agents and *real estate brokers* work for property owners, selling, renting, or managing their property.

Service sales representatives sell services such as cable television, telephone communications systems, hotel accommodations, data processing, advertising, printing, and management consulting.

Travel agents help individuals plan trips. They arrange for air, ship, rail, or bus transportation, make hotel and motel reservations, arrange for tours and car rentals, and generally help their customers plan their vacations.

Educational Requirements

Educational requirements vary, depending on the product or service the individual sells. College degrees are not necessary for most types of retail and wholesale sales work. But manufacturers' sales representatives should have a degree in a field related to the products they sell. A representative for an aircraft manufacturer, for example, should have a degree in aeronautical engineering so that he can converse intelligently with prospective buyers.

Similarly, financial services and securities sales representatives would be better served by obtaining a college degree in business administration, economics, finance, or liberal arts. In most states they must be licensed and registered. They must pass the General Securities Registered Representative Examination, as well as the National Uniform Securities Agents State Law Examination.

Insurance companies also prefer individuals with college degrees, particularly if they are in business or economics. Computer literacy is also an important prerequisite in this field. Most insurance sales workers must be licensed by the state in which they work. Real estate agents and brokers must also pass a written examination and be licensed by the state, but it is easier to get into this field than into insurance with only a high school education.

For many selling jobs, such as that of travel agent, new employees are trained in the classroom or on the job. The training period varies from one month to two years or more.

School Subjects

Basic courses in marketing, advertising, sales, communications, accounting, computers, purchasing, psychology, business practices, and economics would benefit all individuals who are seeking a career in sales. Beyond that, the individual should take courses related to his or her specific area of interest. Someone interested in becoming a financial services sales representative, for example, should take courses in business administration, budget management; financial analysis, data processing, managerial finance, and money and banking. And someone interested in selling computers should take courses in computer science.

Aptitudes

Whether a salesperson is selling to retail customers or to purchasing agents for a corporation, whether he or she is selling clothing, computers, or coffee, selling is a people-oriented profession.

The common traits found among all successful salespersons are enthusiasm, self-confidence, and, most importantly, the desire and ability to get along with others. To sell effectively, you must be able to deal with other individuals—to communicate with them. As a result, an objective score in personality on the word association test is important, because this indicates an ability to function well in—and to enjoy—a career that involves almost constant interaction with people.

Ideaphoria, the ability to produce a rapid flow of ideas, is perhaps the most important aptitude a salesperson can possess, for it enables the individual to be creative in his or her sales approach. Going hand-in-hand with high ideaphoria is a score in structural visualization that is not high, for this indicates that the individual is more comfortable in the world of words than in the world of concrete things. An exception to this would be the field of sales engineering, which involves the selling of aeronautical, agricultural, electrical, electronic, mechanical, mining, and other technical products. High structural visualization, the ability to picture in one's mind the structure of three-dimensional forms, enables the individual to look at a blueprint and visualize what the finished product will look like and how the various elements of the product fit together. A sales engineer who possesses this trait is best able to handle technical questions and to offer technical advice to customers.

144

SCIENTIST, RESEARCH

Job Description

The work of research scientists is extremely varied and depends upon their area of specialization. Research scientists generally fall into two broad categories: life scientists and physical scientists. Each of these two categories may be broken down into a number of specialties, and these specialties may be further broken down into many subspecialties. Life scientists, for example, include agricultural scientists and biological scientists. Physical scientists include chemists, geologists, geophysicists, meteorologists, physicists, and astronomers. The work entailed in these specialties, and their many subspecialties, is detailed below.

LIFE SCIENTISTS

Agricultural scientists devise ways to improve the quantity and quality of farm animals and farm crops in order to raise agricultural productivity. Among the areas of specialization open to agricultural scientists are: agronomy (the study of soil management and how crops grow); animal science (research into the breeding, feeding, and health of farm animals); apiculture (the study of the breeding and care of bees); entomology (the study of insects and their relationship to humans and plant and animal life); horticulture (the study and improvement of fruits, vegetables, and greenhouse and nursery crops; and soil science (the study of soil characteristics).

Biological scientists study living organisms, their life processes, and their relationship to their environment. Among the areas of specialization for biologists are: aquatic biology (the study of plants and animals that live in water); biochemistry (the study of the chemical composition of living things); botany (the study of plants and their relationship to their environment; ecology (the study of the interrelationship of organisms and their environments); microbiology (the study of such microscopic organisms as bacteria and viruses); physiology (the study of the activities and life functions of animals and plants); and zoology (the study of the origin, behavior, diseases, and life processes of animals).

PHYSICAL SCIENTISTS

Chemists investigate and put to practical use knowledge about chemicals. Areas of specialization within the field of chemistry are:

145

analytical chemistry (the study and identification of the structure, composition, and nature of chemical substances); biochemistry (the study of the chemical compounds of living things); inorganic chemistry (the study of compounds consisting of elements other than carbon); organic chemistry (the study of carbon compounds); and physical chemistry (the study of the physical characteristics of chemical substances and how chemical reactions work).

Geologists and *geophysicists* study the origin, history, and structure of the earth. Among the many areas of specialization in this field are: geochemical oceanography (the study of the chemical composition of the oceans and the dissolved elements and nutrients there); geological oceanography (the study of the ocean floor); hydrology (the study of properties, distribution, and circulation of underground and surface waters); meteorology (the study of the earth's atmosphere and weather); mineralogy (the study of minerals and precious stones); paleontology (the study of fossils found in geological formations in order to trace the evolution of plant and animal life and the geologic history of the earth); and physical oceanography (the study of currents and other physical characteristics of the ocean).

Physicists investigate the basic principles governing the structure and behavior of matter, the generation and transfer of energy, and the interaction of matter and energy. Among the areas of specialization in this field are: atomic and molecular physics; elementary particle physics; nuclear physics; and plasma physics.

Astronomers study the universe and such celestial bodies as the sun, moon, planets, stars, and galaxies.

Educational Requirements

The federal government and some other institutions hire research scientists who have only a master's degree, but generally a Ph.D. is required in the specific discipline or a closely related discipline. For a position as an agricultural research scientist, for example, the individual may obtain a Ph.D. in agricultural science, but a Ph.D. in biology is also acceptable to many employers, provided the individual has taken course work or done field work in agricultural science. Ph.D.'s in all disciplines, from astronomy to zoology, require field work and/or laboratory research and a thesis or dissertation, as well as classroom work.

146

College Subjects

Those who hope to pursue a career as a research scientist should complete as many science, mathematics, and computer courses as possible. In addition, courses must be taken in one's area of specialization. Research chemists, for example, should take such courses as analytical, organic, and inorganic chemistry. Meteorologists need to study atmospheric science and weather analysis and forecasting. And physicists must study such subjects as thermodynamics and molecular physics.

Aptitudes

An important aptitude for scientists is structural visualization. Structural visualization, the ability to picture in one's mind the structure of three-dimensional forms, enables the scientist to look at a blueprint, technical drawing, or plan of something and picture how it will look when it is built. It is especially helpful to those scientists who design and construct laboratory equipment, testing apparatuses, and other scientific equipment. Research physicists, for example, design lasers, telescopes, and cyclotrons, and research chemists help design chemical manufacturing facilities and the advanced equipment that goes into them. In addition, high structural visualization is an asset to those scientists who examine the structure of atoms, molecules, and crystals. It is also useful in mathematics, and mathematical skills are essential in all areas of scientific research.

Inductive reasoning, the ability to reason from the particular to the general and to form a conclusion, is also helpful. This trait enables the scientist to conduct a variety of tests and experiments and to develop a theory based on the data collected. It also comes into play in problem-solving, enabling the research scientist to see what is wrong with a particular experimental process, why it is wrong, and to provide solutions.

For the most part, the work of a research scientist is of an individual nature, with the scientist spending much time in a laboratory, where he or she conducts research, tests and experiments, or in an office, where he or she plans, records, and reports on the research. As a result, this field would be appropriate for the individual who scores subjective in personality on the word-association test—an indication that he or she prefers work of an individual nature.

147

SOCIOLOGIST

Job Description

Sociologists study the individuals, groups, and institutions that make up human society. They conduct research into the structure, development, and behavior of such societal groups as families, tribes, gangs, communities, governments, and religions. They collect and analyze data on social classes, ethnic minorities, and social institutions, and on social change and other social phenomena.

Sociologists study group origins, growth, activities, and trends. They study institutions such as schools and churches, and determine their roles in shaping social groups. They also coordinate research on development, consequences of acceptable and deviant behavior, political and economic customs, and other fundamental differences of groups. Sociologists use this information to determine the effect that groups have on the overall function of society. They also formulate data to help to explain the causes of crime, poverty, and other societal problems.

Many sociologists work as social workers, counselors, and teachers. Others act as consultants to administrators, lawmakers, or other authorities that deal with social policy, and are active in such areas as health, welfare, poverty, and population studies. Some of the branches of sociology are detailed below.

Criminologists study crime, including its causes, correction, and prevention.

Demographers study the size, composition, growth, and movement of populations.

Environmental sociologists study the effects of the environment on people.

Gerontologists study aging and the problems faced by aged individuals.

Medical sociologists study the social factors that affect the health of individuals and groups.

Social organization sociologists study the origin, development, activities, and interaction of such social groups as the family, tribe, and community.

Urban sociologists study life in cities and other densely populated areas.

Educational Requirements

A four-year bachelor of arts degree in sociology. Many graduate sociologists then go on to take a two-year master's program. A seven- or eight-year Ph.D. program in sociology is required for teaching or research positions in colleges and universities. A Ph.D. is also essential for senior-level positions in government agencies, consulting firms, research institutes, and corporations.

College Subjects

Sociological theory; social psychology; statistics; English; economics; social statistics and quantitative methods; crime and deviance; family and society; population; urban and rural sociology; social organizations; sociology of the arts, education, law, mental health, politics, religion, science and technology, and work.

Aptitudes

The Foundation believes that the individual with inductive reasoning, the ability to reason from the particular to the general and to draw an inference, would find scope for this trait in sociology. Like physicians and counselors, sociologists must be able to take a set of facts and develop a theory that explains them. That is, they must be able to utilize their research findings to develop practical solutions. For example, a sociologist who specializes in social organization, might study families to discover the causes of, say, alcoholism, and then utilize his or her findings to help devise a substance-abuse program.

Low or average structural visualization is also an important asset for sociologists, because it indicates that the individual is more likely to enjoy working in a field that involves the use of words rather than in a profession where concrete things are most important. And if you possess high ideaphoria and have an interest in teaching, this profession would offer you an outlet for your ideaphoria.

The field of sociology offers many opportunities for those who score either objective or subjective in personality on the word-association test. A person who scores objective might prefer working as part of a team. Teamwork is quite prevalent in sociology because people from many different disciplines are often needed to solve social problems. A person who scores subjective will find many opportunities to do individual research work.

149

SURVEYOR

Job Description

Surveyors measure the size, shape, or location of any part of the earth's surface, including mountains, valleys, islands, rivers, lakes, and oceans. The area they measure can be as small as a plot of land for a home or as large as a the entire surface of the earth.

Their surveys helps determine land, water, and real estate boundaries, the proper laying out of highways and other engineering works, and the precise renditions of maps and charts. Surveys are also used for the drawing of hydrographic charts used for navigating waterways; for aeronautical charts; and for the drawing of geological maps and soil survey maps, which are of use to mining companies.

In their work, surveyors use a variety of tools and instruments to measure distances, elevations, and angles. These include a tape measure, for measuring distances; a special type of telescope, called a level, for measuring differences in heights; and a transit, another special type of telescope that can measure angles. Many different kinds of electronic equipment and systems are also used in surveying. The Global Positioning System (GPS), for example, is an electronic system that uses information from satellites to precisely locate points on the earth's surface.

Surveyors work for construction, mining, and oil-extraction companies, engineering and architectural firms, surveying companies, and federal, state and local government agencies. Federal government agencies that hire surveyors include the Forest Service, Army Corps of Engineers, U.S. Geological Survey, National Geodetic Survey, and Bureau of Land Management.

The type of work entailed in some different areas of surveying is detailed below.

Land surveyors establish official land and water boundaries and measure construction and mineral sites.

Geodetic surveyors measure land areas that are so large that astronautical observations from satellites are necessary in order to determine the land boundaries.

Marine surveyors measure such bodies of water as harbors, rivers, and lakes.

Mine surveyors measure mines, tunnels, and subway sites.

Educational Requirements

One to four years of post-secondary school education in surveying at a technical institute, vocational school, or junior or community college is necessary for advancement in this field. A bachelor's degree in surveying or a related field is becoming increasingly important, and is mandatory in some states.

All 50 states require surveyors to take a state examination to be licensed. To pass this test, an applicant should have some post-secondary school education plus a minimum of five years of on-the-job experience.

College Subjects

Surveying; topography; algebra; geometry; trigonometry; calculus; drafting; mechanical drawing; computer science.

Aptitudes

If you score high in structural visualization—the ability to picture in one's mind the structure of three-dimensional forms—you might be interested in becoming a surveyor. High structural visualization is also useful in mathematics, and mathematical skills are necessary in surveying.

Because much of a surveyor's work involves measurements, the recording of survey results, the verification of data, and the like, average or high graphoria—a measure of one's speed with paper and pencil tasks—is also an important aptitude.

TEACHER

Job Description

The basic job of a teacher is to help people learn the skills and the knowledge that will enable them to lead productive and rewarding lives. Teachers teach in kindergartens, elementary schools, secondary schools, colleges, universities, and adult-education centers. But despite the great differences in the teaching profession at these different levels, there are some aspects of the job—planning, presentation, and evaluation, for example—that are the same or similar.

At each level, the teacher must develop a broad plan of the

material to be taught. The plan is then broken down into teaching units that are spread out over the entire course. These units are broken down further into daily lesson plans.

Lesson material may be presented in a variety of ways. The teacher explains the subject matter to the students, and may then assign further reading and require the students to discuss and write about the subject. At times, the teacher may direct the students to work individually, and at other times to work in groups. The teacher may also use audio-visual aids and take or send the students on field trips.

Teachers must also evaluate the students' progress. One way of doing this is to give written tests, but the students' responses in class and involvement in group discussions also enable the teacher to come to some conclusion about their progress.

Other responsibilities of teachers include the selection of books and other materials to be used in class and the general guidance of students, especially those in elementary and secondary schools. In addition, teachers must be generally well informed about the important issues of the day, even those issues that are not within their specific area of expertise.

The type of work entailed at the different levels of the teaching profession is detailed below.

Kindergarten teachers teach young children who are generally five years of age or younger. Kindergarten, along with nursery school and other programs for pre-elementary-school students, is part of what is known as early-childhood education. Kindergarten teachers prepare youngsters for later education through programs that involve sharing with others, following simple instructions, solving problems, making choices, and developing basic skills. Many of the programs include game-playing, the use of simple tools, story-telling, painting, music, building with blocks, and the enjoyment of plants and other nature materials.

Elementary school teachers introduce children to language, numbers, social studies, and science. They teach basic skills using artwork, music, games, films, slides, and computers. In most elementary schools, one or perhaps two teachers instruct the class in several subjects, although some elementary school teachers may also specialize in and teach only one subject, such as music, art, science, or mathematics.

Secondary school teachers generally teach one subject, such as mathematics, English, or social studies, in junior and senior high schools. In small communities, however, teachers often are expected to teach more than one subject, such as English and history, mathematics and science, or chemistry and biology. They present their course material in lectures and with demonstrations. Audio-visual aids are frequently used in the presentation of material, and computers are being used more and more frequently.

College and university professors teach one or more subjects to students in public and private universities and 2- and 4-year colleges. They present course material to students by way of lectures in large halls, small seminars, or laboratories. They may use such teaching aids as cable and closed-circuit television and computers. Teachers also assist students with academic problems and may also act as counselors and advise students on courses of study. Many also engage in research in their areas of specialty. Individuals who teach at the college and university level generally start out as an instructor and then advance to the higher ranks of assistant professor, associate professor, and full professor.

Vocational and adult-education teachers teach job skills as well as courses that bring personal enrichment. Most vocational and adult-education courses are for those individuals who do not intend to pursue a college degree; they include, for example, courses in woodworking, electrical work, photography, cosmetology, and welding. Other courses include reading, writing, mathematics, and other basic subjects for adults.

Educational Requirements

Kindergarten and elementary school teachers who teach in public schools must be certified by the state in which they teach; the requirements for certification vary from state to state. Generally, certification requires a bachelor's degree and the completion of a teacher education program. Teachers in private schools do not need to be certified by the state.

Secondary school teachers who teach in public schools must be certified by the state in which they teach. Certification requires a bachelor's degree and the completion of a teacher education program; some states require graduate study before the issuance of permanent teaching certification. Teachers in private schools do not need to be certified by the state.

College and university professors: require a master's degree for a beginning job as an instructor. To advance to assistant, associate, or full professor, additional teaching experience, a doctoral degree, and research and publication of papers and books is required.

Vocational and adult-education teachers generally are required to have work experience in their field, though training requirements vary widely from state to state. A bachelor's, master's, or doctoral degree is sometimes required, depending upon the individual's area of specialization. In most states, teachers of adult basic education courses must have teacher certification or a bachelor's degree from a teacher training program.

College Subjects

For teaching at any level, from kindergarten to graduate school, the teacher should either major in education and take courses in his or her field of specialization—science or social studies, for example—or major in his or her field of specialization and take courses in education. Depending upon the level at which one teaches, education courses might include classroom evaluation, the craft of teaching, philosophy of education, psychology of learning, and teaching methods. Clearly, the higher up the scale of education one teaches, the more important it is to take courses in subfields of one's discipline as well as courses covering the entire discipline. For those who teach the youngest students, courses in such subjects as counseling, early childhood education, and child psychology are necessary.

Aptitudes

The teacher's basic job is to teach—to educate students and to help them develop the skills necessary for living and thriving in a complex and competitive world. But despite this basic goal, the profession of teaching is quite varied: the teaching of elementary school students, for example, is very different from the teaching of college students or of adults in adult education classes. As a result, the teaching profession offers interesting opportunities for individuals with differing interests and aptitudes.

You might, for example, consider a career in teaching if you

154

scored high in ideaphoria. It is important for teachers to have an abundant flow of ideas, so that they can stimulate students and keep them interested. They must be able to instill in the students a desire to learn. This is especially true for those teaching in junior-high school and high school. Ideaphoria, however, is not as important to those who teach in colleges or universities, because here students are assumed to be more mature and therefore more inclined to do the work that is required of them. At the college and university level, especially, it is the teacher's knowledge, rather than his or her presentation, that is most important.

For similar reasons, those who score either objective and subjective in personality on the word-association test may consider a career in teaching. Those who are objective—an indication that they enjoy working with and through others—should consider teaching at the pre-college level, because the interaction between teacher and student at this level is more intense than at the college level. A teacher with a subjective personality—an indication that he or she prefers working as an individual—would be more at home teaching adult-education courses or at the college level, where students work more independently or attend lectures in huge auditoriums that may seat hundreds of people. A subjective personality also comes into play when the college or university professor engages in research and writes articles or books for publication.

Low structural visualization is another important trait for most teachers, because this indicates that the individual would be most comfortable in a profession in which the written and oral word are of great importance. An exception would be teachers of woodworking, mechanical drawing, metalworking, and other industrial arts, where high structural visualization would be an asset. Similarly, while the auditory, or sound-related, aptitudes would not be of particular value to most teachers, they would be essential to teachers of music.

UNDERWRITER

Job Description

Underwriters accept, review, and evaluate applications for insurance companies to determine the degree of risk. They assess whether their company should insure the applicant, and, if so, they draft the terms of the contract and quote rates of the premium.

Insurance underwriters first evaluate the application and review medical reports and actuarial tables. They then decide whether to issue a policy. They consider all data relevant to the potential policyholder, including value and condition of property, a person's age, and his or her occupation, medical history, and financial standing.

An important part of an insurance underwriter's work is to determine the cost of the insurance premiums. If the appraisal is too conservative, the client will go elsewhere. If the appraisal is too liberal, excess claims may be paid out. If there is a possibility of a calamity leading to a costly layout by the insurance company, the underwriter will not accept the application.

Most insurance underwriters work in one of three main sections of insurance: health, life, or property and liability. Many underwriters specialize, becoming, for example, casualty underwriters, group underwriters, or special risk underwriters.

Educational Requirements

A four-year bachelor's degree in business administration with experience in accounting is the minimum requirement for positions as underwriters in most insurance companies. Some smaller companies hire individuals without a college degree and enter them into underwriter trainee programs. The trainee programs provide hands-on experience, working with applications, claim files, and actuarial tables.

College Subjects

Financial accounting; computer science; statistics; business administration; managerial accounting; auditing concepts; money and banking; econometrics; probability; actuarial science.

Aptitudes

Speed and accuracy with paper and pencil tasks (high graphoria), as measured by the number-checking test, is an important aptitude for underwriters, because much of their work is with numbers. In addition, number facility—the ability to perform arithmetic operations quickly—is an important aptitude for underwriters because they must use quantitative information to make decisions or recommendations.

156

Underwriters, for example, use actuarial tables and studies in order to determine the costs of insurance premiums.

A low score in structural visualization is another asset for underwriters, because it indicates that the individual is more at home in the world of abstractions than in the world of concrete things.

Scoring subjective in personality on the word-association test would also be helpful to those interested in the underwriting field, because this indicates a preference for working as an individual rather than with or through others. Underwriters sometimes meet with union or employer representatives or accompany insurance salesmen when they visit prospective customers, but for the most part their work involves the perusal of records and actuarial studies, the writing of reports and policies, and other tasks involving an individual effort.

URBAN/REGIONAL PLANNER

Job Description

Urban planners develop programs that provide for the utilization, growth, and revitalization of land, buildings, and other facilities in metropolitan areas. Regional planners develop similar programs for larger areas, such as counties or states; Silicon Valley in California is a well-known product of regional planning.

Urban and regional planners help government officials to make more informed decisions regarding economic, social, and environmental factors directly affecting the city, county, or state. They work with civic leaders, social scientists, and land-development experts to study the current use of land for business, recreational, and residential purposes. They determine the best ways to invest capital in such community services as water and sewer lines and transportation, in the preservation of cultural and recreational sites, and in urban renewal—the redevelopment of city centers. Urban and regional planners are also involved in the building of schools, public housing, and nursing homes.

Urban and regional planners must keep up with changes in environmental regulations and building codes as well as population trends. Another job of the planner is to provide information and suggestions regarding ways of using underutilized or undeveloped land

and facilities. Some planners concentrate on the environmental impact of development projects, others on the physical design of facilities, and still others on the social impact.

Educational Requirements

A four-year bachelor's degree in planning, architecture, or engineering is the minimum requirement for entry-level positions, although most beginning positions in federal, state, and local agencies require two years of work experience or graduate study in regional or urban planning. A master's degree in planning or an MBA or law degree should also be considered by those seeking a career in this field.

The American Institute of Certified Planners grants certification to those individuals who pass an examination and have met the required amount of educational and professional experience.

Because architectural computer programs can be used to view potential development projects, and because computers can be used to record and analyze the vast amount of data compiled in any project, computer skills are becoming increasingly important in urban and regional planning.

College Subjects

Demography; statistical urban studies; sanitary engineering; economics; finance; political science; public administration; location theory; architectural design; structural engineering; computer science; soil mechanics; transportation engineering; law and urban problems; developmental sociology.

Aptitudes

Like architects, urban and regional planners must be able to think in terms of spatial relationships. As a result, structural visualization—the ability to picture in one's mind the structure of three-dimensional forms—is an important aptitude for planners. With high structural visualization, they can picture, for example, how the blueprints and drawings of a plan will translate into a finished and integrated project. In addition, high structural visualization is useful in mathematics, and mathematical skills are important for urban and regional planners.

The ability to remember designs is also a valuable trait. This aptitude helps planners to remember the many different elements—

158

residences, commercial structures, roads, schools, rail lines, and so on—that make up an urban or regional plan. The ability to remember the various elements and aspects of a plan helps planners create structures that fit harmoniously with one another and with the environment.

Ideaphoria—the ability to produce a rapid flow of ideas—is also useful to planners, because they often have to sell their ideas to politicians, legislators, community groups, and others who often have opposing desires and needs. They must be able to influence the choices of these diverse interests

The field of urban and regional planning has opportunities for those who score either subjective or objective in personality on the word-association test. One who scores subjective might prefer work of an individual nature, such as sitting in front of a computer, drafting reports or recording and analyzing information. One who scores objective—an indication that her or she works well with or through others—will find many opportunities to interact with real-estate developers, industry leaders, social scientists, environmentalists, lawyers, transportation officials, and many others.

We have presented here descriptions of a number of occupations. You will find the divisions of each occupational field listed in the catalog of any large university and in other publications to be found in your library. Browsing through the descriptions of courses and occupations will give you a glimpse of the multitude of things that people do. Anything that looks tempting to your aptitudes can be investigated further by looking over the books on that kind of activity or by talking with people who do that kind of work.

The names, locations, and descriptions of schools where you can study for your occupation can be found in books such as *Guide to College Majors*, *Lovejoy's College Guide*, *Lovejoy's Career and Vocational School Guide*, or *The College Blue Book*, to be found in most libraries.

If you are slow in paper and pencil work, you will fare better at one of the smaller schools where the usually smaller classes are conducive to more spoken and less written interplay between teacher and student.

Your vocabulary size can be related not to the size of the college but to its age. Many institutions gradually raise their standards as they become established and gain prestige. *The College Handbook*, published by the College Entrance Examination Board, lists more than 2,000 two-year and four-year colleges, with the verbal scores of their applicants and accepted students. Select a school where the majority of students are at about your level.

A story is told of a boarding school where the students were segregated by grade level in the dining room as well as in the classrooms, with those in each grade sitting at a separate table. On becoming conscious of vocabulary, the school tried an experiment of seating at each table the students with similar vocabulary levels, regardless of grade. The effect was amazing. Faces brightened, conversation was enlivened, and discipline problems decreased. You have more fun with people who speak your own language.

The purpose of what you have been reading will have been realized if the recurring references to vocabulary are heard by you as variations on a pleasant melodic theme that you are unable to forget, and if you can employ more fully your own combination of aptitudes in a satisfying way.

INDEX

Accordion playing, 58-59
Accounting, 59, 69-71
  aptitude test, 19-20
  cost accounting, 61
  financial managers, 108
  hotel managers, 121
  ideaphoria, 4
  musical aptitudes, 36
  number facility, 26
  three-dimensional thinking, 6
  visual perception, 20
Accounting Aptitude test, 19-20
  See also Graphoria
Acoustical engineering, 105
  aptitude patterns, 56
  musical aptitudes, 37
Actuary, 71-73
Administration
  civil engineers, 105
  general managers, 120-123
  ideaphoria, 4
  nurses, 126
  physicians, 131
  See also Management
Administrative services manager,
  73-75
Admiralty law, 116
Adult-education teachers, 153-155
Advertising
  account executives, 75-77
  art directors, 77-78
  copywriters, 76, 78-80
  design memory, 31
  ideaphoria, 3
  marketing managers, 124, 125
  musical aptitudes, 36
  property managers, 134
  public relations workers, 139
Aeronautical drafting, 99
Aeronautical engineering, 103

Aerospace engineering, 103
Age
  decline of inductive reasoning and,
    55-56
  maturity of aptitudes and, 36
  three-dimensional thinking and, 6
Agricultural economists, 66
Agricultural engineering, 61, 103
Agriculture, 61-62
  research scientists, 145
Agronomy, 145
Air-conditioning systems,
  installation of, 89
Air Force personnel, color blindness
  in, 31
Air pollution, control of, 64
Allergists, 132
Aluminum manufacturers, 54
American Bar Association, 117
American Institute of Certified
  Planners, 158
American Institute of Interior
  Design, 98
American Occupational Therapy
  Certification Board, 129
Analytical chemistry, 64, 146
Analytical reasoning
  actuaries, 72, 73
  editors, 101, 102
  printers, 68
Anesthesiology
  nurses, 126
  physicians, 132
Animal-science research, 145
Annuity contracts, 71
Anthropology, 62-63
Apiculture, 62, 145
Apparent Movement test, 22
Appraisers, in farm-related
  businesses, 61
Apprenticeships
  drafters, 100
  furniture designers, 97
  pre-Industrial Revolution, 9
Aptitude patterns, 53-57

161

Aptitudes
  acquired abilities and, 6
  age of maturity of, 36
  distracting, 36, 37
  diversity of, in single occupation,
    53-57
  independence of, 57
  inheritance of. *See* Inheritance,
    aptitude
  interests and, 49-52
  occupation analysis in terms of,
    58-59
  presence of, and learning handicaps,
    10, 11
  supplementary, 37
  unused, 1, 5, 11, 54, 56
  use of, 1, 5
  See also specific aptitudes
Aptitude tests, 1, 60
  development of, 4, 5
  discoveries in history of testing,
    54, 57
  high scores on, 4
  improvement of scores on, 13
  low scores on, 4
  See also specific aptitudes and
    specific aptitude tests
Archaeology, 62, 80-82
Architect Registration Examination,
  83
Architectural engineering, 103
Architecture, 82-84
  construction managers, 90
  design memory, 31
  drafters, 99
  musical aptitudes, 37
  surveyors, 150
  three-dimensional thinking,
    7, 10, 24
Archivists, 84-86
Army Corps of Engineers
  surveyors, 150
Art, 30-32, 63
  advertising art directors, 77-78
  design memory, 14

dexterity, 13
  dress designers, 36-37
  medical and scientific illustrators,
    109-110
  numerical traits, 27
  printers, 68
  three-dimensional designers, 7, 49,
    96-99
Art history, 86-87
Art librarians, 120
Assembly workers
  dexterity, 12, 13, 60
  ideaphoria, 1
Astronomy
  mathematics, 67
  research scientists, 146
  three-dimensional thinking, 6
Atomic physics, 146
Atomic research, 63
Auction work, 27
Audiovisual services managers, 74
Auditing, 69
  ideaphoria, 4
  visual perception, 20
Auditory aptitudes, 14, 33-38, 56
  acoustical engineers, 105
  entertainment lawyers, 118
  general managers, 123
  psychologists, 138
  teachers, 155
  See also Music, careers in
Automobile mechanics, 8
Automotive drafting, 99

Bacteriology, 68
Banking
  bank officers, 87-89
  financial managers, 107-108
  financial services sales
    representatives, 143
  ideaphoria, 4
  lawyers, 116
  number facility, 26
  tellers, 7, 26
  three-dimensional thinking, 6, 7

Beekeeping. *See* Apiculture
Behavioral science. *See* Psychology
Biochemistry, 48, 64
  research scientists, 145, 146
Biology, 64
  atomic research, 63
  ideaphoria, 4
  mathematics, 67
  medical and scientific illustrators,
    109-110
  research scientists, 145
  three-dimensional thinking, 6
  zoology, 68-69
Biomedical engineers, 103
Biophysics, 64
Blueprint drawing and reading, 93
  cost estimators, 94
  drafters, 100
  engineering technicians, 107
  engineers, 104
  patent lawyers, 118
  research scientists, 147
  urban and regional planners, 158
Bookkeeping
  cost accounting, 61
  ideaphoria, 4
  idle aptitudes, 54
  numerical traits, 26, 27
  perceptual speed, 19
Botany, 145
Bricklayers, 91
Broadcast journalism, 114
Brokerage office managers, 121
Budgeting
  construction managers, 90, 91
  financial managers, 108
  industrial production managers, 110
  librarians, 119, 120
Building
  clergy, 65
  urban and regional planners, 157
  See also Construction
Building plans, use of, 93
Burger, Warren, 18
Business careers

financial managers, 108
general managers, 123
ideaphoria, 4
law, 116
librarians, 119
number facility, 26
objective persons, 15
subjective persons, 15-16
three-dimensional thinking, 6
vocabulary, 44

CAD. *See* Computer-aided drafting
    systems
California Polytechnic State
    University, 3-4
  academic standards, 9
  Clerical and Perceptual Speed test,
    20
  number-comparison test, 21-22
Camouflage, color blindness and,
    31, 32
Cardiology, 132
Career counseling, 95
Career development, 58
Carpentry, 90, 91
  construction managers, 89
Cartography, 67
Cartooning, 63
Cash managers, 108
Casualty underwriters, 156
Certified public accountants, 70
Chemical engineering, 103
Chemical engineering technicians,
    106
Chemistry, 53, 64-65
  atomic research, 63
  mathematics, 67
  research scientists, 145, 146
  soil, 62
  three-dimensional thinking, 6
Children
  interests, widening of, 49-50
  maturity of aptitudes in, 36
  musical aptitudes, 33
  vocabulary building, 39, 42-44

164

Contract administration managers, 74
Copyediting, 102
Copywriter, advertising, 76, 78-80
Corporate law, 116
Correspondence work, 73
Cost accounting, 61, 70
Cost estimating, 93-94
  construction managers, 90
Costume designing, 37
Counseling, 94-96
  psychologists, 137
  sociologists, 148
CPA. *See* Certified public accountants
Craftsmen, dexterity of, 13
Creative imagination. *See* Ideaphoria
Credit card operations managers, 108
Credit managers, farm-related businesses, 61
Criminal lawyers, 116
Criminology, 148
Critical thinking. *See* Inductive reasoning
Critical writing, 17
Cultural anthropology, 62
Customer service, in banking, 88

Data processing, 73
DAT Clerical Speed and Accuracy subtest, 23
Defense attorneys, 116
Demography, 148
  numerical traits, 27
Dental Aptitude Test, 66
Dentistry, 65-66
  assistants, 66
  dexterity, 13, 49
  hygienists, 66
  laboratory technicians, 66
Dermatology, 132
Design engineering, 105
Designing
  advertising art directors, 77
  subjective persons, 15

three-dimensional, 96-99
Design memory, 8, 14, 30
  advertising art directors, 78
  archaeologists, 81, 82
  architects, 83, 84
  art historians, 87
  art librarians, 120
  engineers, 105
  general managers, 123
  geologists, 55
  medical and scientific illustrators, 110
  printers, 68
  three-dimensional designing, 98, 99
  urban and regional planners, 158
Detectives. *See* Law enforcement
Developmental psychology, 137
Dexterity, 12-14
  artistic fields, 30
  low, 49
    music abilities and, 37
  See also Finger dexterity; Tweezer dexterity
Dexterity tests, 60
Diagnosticians
  clergy, 65
  inductive reasoning, 17
Diagnostic thinking. *See* Inductive reasoning
Diplomacy, 17
Distracting aptitudes, 1, 36, 37, 57
Divorce law, 116
Doctors. *See* Physicians
Drafting, 99-100
  architects, 84
Drawing
  drafters, 99
  medical and scientific illustrators, 109-110
  three-dimensional thinking, 7
  See also Art
Dress designing. *See* Fashion designing
Drummers, rhythm memory in, 35
Drywall workers, 92

165

Females
clerical and perceptual speed, 20-21
color blindness, 31
number checking, 21
perceptual speed, 23
three-dimensional thinking, 7, 10
Finance
accountants, 71
farm-related businesses, 61
numerical traits, 27
Financial analysis, numerical traits
used in, 26-27
Financial economists, 66
Financial manager, 107-108
Financial planning, numerical traits
used in, 27
Financial records, processing of, 73
Financial services sales
representatives, 143, 144
Finger dexterity, 12-14
art, 63
low
accordion playing, 59
singers, 36
occupational therapists, 129
petroleum geologists, 55
printers, 68
three-dimensional thinking and, 7, 8
Finger-dexterity test, 3, 12, 13
Finish carpentry, 91
Flicker Fusion test, 22
Floor-covering installers, 92
Floral designing, 97
Food-service managers. *See*
Restaurant and food-service
managers
Foreign languages
auditory abilities, 34
bank officers, 88
nonsense syllables, memorization
of, 35
three-dimensional thinking, 6,
10, 11
Forensic psychology, 137
Forest Service, U.S., surveyors, 150

Freelance workers
copywriters, 80
editors, 101
Fund-raising
clergy, 65
public relations workers, 139
Furniture designing, 96-98

Gastroenterology, 132
General contractors, 89-91
General Electric Company, 2
Accounting Aptitude test, 19
finger dexterity, 12, 13
testing practices, 60
General Securities Registered
Representative Examination, 143
Genetics, use of, in agriculture, 62
Geochemical oceanography, 146
Geodesy, 68
Geodetic surveyors, 150
Geography, 67
Geological Survey, U.S., 150
Geology, 146
aptitude patterns, 55-57
geological engineers, 103
idle aptitudes, use of, 56
oceanography, 146
petroleum industry, 53-56
Geophysics, 56, 146
Geriatric nurses, 126
Gerontology, 148
Glaziers, 92
Global Positioning System, 150
Government workers
accountants, 69
archivists, 85
cost estimators, 93
economists, 66
geographers, 67
lawyers, 115, 116, 118
librarians, 119
public relations workers, 139-140
surveyors, 150
urban and regional planners, 157
vocabulary levels of, 43

169

Mechanical engineering technicians, 106, 107
Mechanical knowledge tests, 60
Mechanics
atomic research, 63
automobile, 8
Media planners, advertising, 76
Medical and health services
biomedical engineers, 103
health psychologists, 137
health-services managers, 121, 122
inductive reasoning, 17
medical illustrators, 109-110
medical sociologists, 148
numerical traits, 27
nursing, 125-127
occupational therapists, 127-129
physicians, 131-134
specialization, 46
Medieval archaeology, 81
Memory, 28
insight and, 35
librarians, 120
music, 37
for nonsense syllables, 34-35
See also Design memory; Number memory; Rhythm memory; Tonal memory
Mental health field
counseling, 95, 96
occupational therapy, 128
psychologists, 136
Metallurgical engineering, 103
Metallurgical research, 63
Meteorology, 146, 147
Microbiology, 145
Military personnel
color perception, 31-32
geographers, 67
musical traits, 34
Mineralogy, 146
Mining
engineers, 103
surveyors, 150
of uranium-bearing ores, 63

Minnesota Clerical Test, 21
Minnesota Paper Form Board test, 8
Missionaries, 65
Molecular physics, 146
Money earnings, vocabulary and, 44
Morphology, 69
Motion pictures
librarians, 119
set designers, 97
MPRE. *See* Multistate Professional Responsibility Examination
MSEE. *See* Multistate Essay Examination
Multistate Bar Examination, 117
Multistate Essay Examination, 117
Multistate Professional Responsibility Examination, 117
Muscles
individual variations in, 47
muscle memory, 35
Museum work
art historians, 86
design memory, 30
exhibition designers, 97
general managers, 123
Music, careers in
accordion playing, 59
auditory aptitudes, 14, 33-38, 56
critics, 37
design memory, 30
directors, religious, 65
general managers, 123
librarians, 120
numerical traits, 27
perceptual speed, 25
teachers, 155

National Board for Certified Counselors, 95
National Board of Medical Examiners, 133
National Board of Osteopathic Medical Examiners, 133
National Certified Counselor, 95
National Counselor Examination, 95

interests and choice of, 50
mental images of, 51
single occupation, diversity of
aptitudes in, 53-57
Oceanography, 146
O'Connor, Johnson, 2
finger-dexterity test, 12, 13
three-dimensional thinking, 8
Office managers, 129-131
Office nurses, 126, 127
Office Worker Test, 19
Ophthalmology, 132
Oral pathology, 66
Oral surgery, 66
Organic chemistry, 64, 146
Ornithology, 69
Orthodontics, 66
Orthopedics, 132
Osteopathy, 131
Otolaryngology, 132

Packaging design, 77, 97
Painting (artistic field)
design memory, 30
dexterity, 13
three-dimensional thinking, 63
visual and tactual discrimination, 14
Painting (construction trade), 92
Paleontology, 146
Paper and Pencil Speed test, 19
Paper-and-pencil work
clerical and perceptual speed,
10, 20, 24
number memory and, 29
numerical problem-solving, 27
record-keeping, 60
See also Graphoria
Paperhanging, 92
Parasitology, 69
Patent drafting, 99-100
Patent law, 116, 118
Pathology, 69, 132
Pediatrics
nurses, 126
physicians, 132

Pedodontics, 66
Pension plans
actuaries, 71
Perceptual speed, 19-25
See also Clerical and perceptual
speed
Periodontics, 66
Personal credit institutions
bank officers, 87
Personality psychologists, 137
Personnel work
counselors, 95
managers, 121
office managers, 130
records, processing of, 73
recruitment, 71
Petroleum industry
engineers, 103
geologists, 53-55
surveyors, 150
Philosophy
clergy, 65
three-dimensional thinking, 10
Photogrammetry, 67
Photography, 30
Photojournalism, 114
Physical anthropology, 62
Physical attributes
individual differences in, 47-48
musical abilities and, 35-36
Physical chemistry, 64, 146
Physical geography, 67
Physical oceanography, 146
Physical scientists, 145-146
Physicians, 131-134
musical traits, 34
numerical traits, 27
Physics
atomic research, 63
mathematics, 67
musical traits, 34
research scientists, 146, 147
three-dimensional thinking, 6,
10, 11
Physiological psychology, 137

175

176

177

179

180